A BEGINNER'S GUIDE TO Hand-Printing

Stylish step-by-step projects using stamps, stencils, screen-printing, and more

CICO BOOKS

Published in 2026 by CICO Books
An imprint of Ryland Peters & Small Ltd
20–21 Jockey's Fields
London WC1R 4BW
1452 Davis Bugg Road
Warrenton, NC 27589
www.rylandpeters.com
Email: euregulations@rylandpeters.com

10 9 8 7 6 5 4 3 2 1

The text and projects in this book have previously appeared in *The Hand Printed Home* and *Handprint and Make Your Own Bags*.

A CIP record for this book is available from the British Library.

US Library of Congress CIP data has been applied for.

ISBN: 978 1 80065 578 2

Printed in China

Editors: Lindsay Kaubi and Hilary Mandelberg
Designer: Geoff Borin
Photographers: Emma Mitchell and Claire Richardson
Stylists: Tanya Goodwin, Nel Haynes, and Carol Wortley
Illustrators: Step-by-step illustrations by Carrie Hill, templates by Stephen Dew and Simon Roulstone

In-house editor: Jenny Dye
Art director: Sally Powell
Creative director: Leslie Harrington
Head of production: Patricia Harrington
Publishing manager: Carmel Edmonds

The authorized representative in the EEA is
Authorised Rep Compliance Ltd.,
Ground Floor. 71 Lower Baggot Street,
Dublin, D01 P593, Ireland
www.arccompliance.com

contents

introduction

Printing by hand can be so much fun, and it's easier than you think to turn everyday things around the home into your own unique creations. Your hand-printed designs can be applied to almost any surface—fabric, paper, ceramics, even your walls—and you don't always need any expensive specialist equipment.

This book contains 35 step-by-step projects that are designed to introduce you to lots of different hand-printing techniques. You'll find a selection of simple print motifs combined with easy sewing projects, as well as some upcycling ideas, and all the information you need to help you get started. You will soon be developing new skills and producing beautiful finished home accessories, decorations, gifts, and bags.

As you work, allow time to test out the prints before you start on the final piece. Remember, though, that the beauty of hand-printing lies in its imperfections and happy accidents, so give yourself time to play and let the designs develop. As with most creative processes, making mistakes is an important way to learn.

Hopefully, you will reach a point where you will be inspired to use your new skills to create your own designs. At that stage, it is worth knowing that you can achieve great designs just by using humble household objects such as potato mashers or rolling pins as your starting points.

As you get into hand-printing, enjoy experimenting and seeing a simple shape become an amazing design. And if you sometimes you get that "blank canvas fear," just start making marks on a piece of paper. Your unique design will soon emerge.

Whether you are a complete novice without any knowledge of the techniques involved, or already have lots of creative experience, this book will be a great starting point. But whichever category of reader you are, just play and have fun with printing and sewing.

practical advice

When choosing fabrics for the projects, look for natural fabrics like canvas, calico, cottons, and linens. They are all are strong and hardwearing, and are easy to print and sew. For most of the bag projects you will need a strong fabric; even for the more delicate bags, you still need a fabric that will hold its shape and not rip if you put your keys inside.

Most projects include some sewing to make up the final items, so for these you will need the basic sewing equipment on page 110.

Before you begin printing, make sure you have a large flat surface to work on and always cover it with plenty of protective material, such as old newspaper, a plastic tablecloth, cut-up plastic refuse sacks, or an old shower curtain. Printing can get a bit messy.

Each of the projects has a skill rating, from Beginner (one circle) to Intermediate (two circles) and Advanced (three circles). The skill levels are based on how complex the project is to print, sew, and make up. Start with the Beginner projects, then move on to the next two levels as you build up your skills and confidence.

design and inspiration

Print motifs are provided for many of the projects (see page 115), but you could also create your own. Look around you and see the patterns that are everywhere. Check out high-street stores and fashion and interior magazines, and look in thrift stores for vintage fabrics, wallpapers, ceramics, books, and magazines. Collect images, color swatches, sketches, and doodles. Find leaves, flowers, and objects, and take photos of shadows, shapes, and architecture—look at the big scene and the tiny details. There is pattern everywhere—you just need to look for it. These will all get your inspiration juices flowing.

mood boards

A mood board is a great way to keep all of your inspiration in one place, so that you can see what ideas develop. A mood board can be a physical board with images pinned to it or a digital file with all of your images collected together.

sketchbooks

If you keep a sketchbook and spend a lot of time playing and drawing in it, the ideas will flow. Draw with different media—pencils, paintbrushes, sticks dipped in ink; the experimentation will help you to find new shapes and marks that will end up as your print designs.

color

Experiment with color. Have a color wheel to hand so you can see the relationship between all the different colors, then try mixing your own fabric paints. Start by mixing just small amounts, noting down the ratios of each color that you have used.

Next, try out your color on the fabric you plan to use for your project. The color of the fabric has a habit of changing the color of the paint, especially once it's dry and ironed.

Once you have the perfect color, scale things up to make the amount you need for your project.

experimenting

Ready to print? As well as using printing blocks made from your own designs, experiment by printing with found objects and layering these prints with your carved block prints to see what magic you can create.

Keep playing. The best designs appear from experimenting and just trying things out. For instance, try layering different colors, or repeating motifs in different ways. Use a mix of techniques—there's nothing to stop you having a base layer of shapes printed with a foam block and a detail layer screen-printed over the top. The more you play, the more you'll be inspired.

pattern types

When you are coming up with your designs, consider whether your print is going to be a repeated pattern or a single motif. Are you going to build up a pattern randomly or have a regular, square repeat? Consider the scale of the design and how it will be spaced out on the fabric. All of these decisions will influence your final designs.

Square repeat

Half-drop repeat

Brick repeat

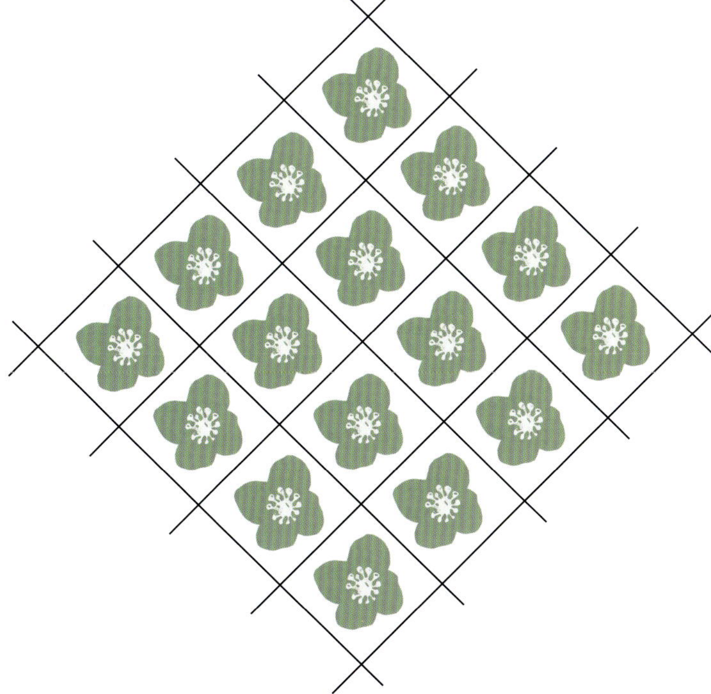

Diamond repeat

Scales repeat

hand-printing techniques

You can put your print design onto blocks, plates, rollers, stamps, or stencils. When deciding what to use, consider the size of the design and whether you are likely to need to make other things with the print. Stencils will only last a short time and then need to be re-made, whereas rubber stamps, if cared for, will last for hundreds of prints. Each technique has its pros and cons, and you will also have your own favorite that you choose to use the most.

Don't be afraid to have a go, and remember that mistakes and imperfections add to the beauty and unique nature of hand-printed items.

basic printing equipment

- Acrylic paint and acrylic fabric medium
- Old jars or plastic pots for mixing and storing paint
- Variety of paintbrushes
- Apron
- Sharp scissors
- Craft knife
- Cutting board
- Newspaper
- Clean cloths
- Plenty of sponges, cut into small squares
- Sponge rollers/brayers
- Masking tape
- Pencil
- Tracing paper
- Hairdryer
- Iron
- Water
- Large flat surface for printing—flat with no lumps

fabric paints

There are many different brands of fabric paint on the market. Some can be too runny to print with and lots come in tiny small bottles, which works out very expensive for large projects. Ask at your local art shop for advice on the best fabric paint for printing.

A versatile way to work is by mixing standard acrylic artists' paints with acrylic fabric medium, which is available in any art-and-craft store. You mix the fabric medium 50:50 with your acrylic paint—and you've got fabric paint! The resulting paint goes further and produces a softer finish on the fabric. It also means that the fabric can be washed. This technique is suitable for all the projects in the book—block printing, stencils, and screen-printing.

All fabric paints, including those made with acrylic fabric medium, must be heat-set with an iron to fix them. Two minutes with a hot iron will usually be enough.

printing with objects from around the house

You can print with just about anything from around your home. Think back to your schooldays, when you made hand- and vegetable prints, and prints using seashells and pasta. The projects are designed to remind you of what's possible, then you can experiment and hopefully, come up with some exciting new designs.

fruit and vegetable prints

You can use lots of different vegetables to make prints with—think of the interesting contours you get when you cut an apple widthwise or a pepper lengthwise or widthwise. Fruit and vegetable printing is one of many forms of relief printing. You create a surface with raised areas that you cover with paint and print—these are the positive parts of the design—and you leave cut-away areas that remain unpainted and unprinted—the negative parts of the design.

The humble potato is one of the most versatile vegetables to use for printing because you can easily carve it to shape.

how to potato print

Cut a potato that is the right size for your project in half, width- or lengthwise, depending on your design. This will give you two surfaces to print with. Draw your motif onto the surface with a marker pen and cut away the areas that you don't need using a craft knife. You must cut downward at least ½in (1cm) into the surface to make sure your finished print has good, crisp edges. Pat the cut surface of your potato dry with kitchen paper, then sponge on the paint and press the potato onto the fabric to make your print. Remove carefully, reapply the paint, and you're ready to print again.

household items

Think of the way a coffee cup leaves a ring on your table. That's a print! Cardboard toilet-paper tubes, cookie cutters, and kitchen utensils like vegetable mashers or whisks all make interesting prints, too. Or you can use a wallpaper roller or rolling pin as your starting point.

how to print with household items

For a print from a household item that already has a sharp edge or a textured surface, simply dip the appropriate part of the item in fabric paint or apply the paint with a sponge, then you are ready to print. Clean the paint thoroughly off the household item after use.

Alternatively, you can cover a roller with shapes cut from foam sheets with a peel-off sticky backing (see the Japanese fabric giftwrap on page 50), or you can wrap the roller in string. Apply the paint with a sponge and whizz the roller across the surface to create a random striped print or a pattern that's a mesh of lines. Experiment, play—and see what you can come up with.

Extras you will need for printing with objects from around the house: Fruits, vegetables, and household items; marker pen; foam sheets with a peel-off sticky backing; string

stamps

You can create reusable stamps for printing from a variety of different materials, such as erasers, foam sheets, and lino. These all use the relief printing technique. You cut the material away to make the positive and negative parts of the design.

The best way to transfer a design onto a stamp is to trace the image onto tracing paper, then place the tracing paper face down on your stamp. Rub the back of the tracing paper and the image will be transferred onto your stamp. The image will now be reversed but once you print it, it will be the correct way around.

carved eraser stamps

Erasers come in all shapes and sizes and provide you with a nice, flexible surface to print from. You can use the shape of the eraser—the dot formed by a pencil eraser or a small eraser, for example—or you can carve a large eraser into the shape and detail you need.

how to use eraser stamps

1 For a carved eraser, mark your design on the surface of the eraser and use a lino cutter and craft knife to cut away the negative areas of the design—the areas that you don't want to print.

2 Cut away the excess eraser from around the design so your finished print has good, crisp edges, but leave enough of the eraser to hold onto from behind.

3 Sponge on the paint and press the eraser stamp onto the fabric to make your print. Carefully remove the eraser stamp and reapply the paint to make the next print.

4 For printing a simple polka-dot design, you can use the eraser on the end of a pencil—it is a ready-made stamp!

Eraser stamps will last a long time if you wash them after use, store them without stacking them on top of one another, and don't try to use them again as erasers.

lino stamps

You can buy sheets of lino in many different sizes from art shops. Invest in a good set of sharp lino-cutting tools; they will make your life easier when it comes to carving your design.

how to use lino stamps

1 Transfer the design onto the piece of lino and carefully carve it out. Use very sharp tools, always cut away from your body, and take great care. Practice on a small piece of lino first if you've never tried lino-cutting before. A good tip is to warm your lino before carving it, as it makes it softer. Sitting on the lino works well!

2 Cut downward to at least half the depth of the lino to make sure your print has crisp edges. You don't need to carve away all the lino around your design; just carve up to ½in (1cm), then cut away the excess using scissors. The raised areas will be covered with paint and printed (the positive parts of the design) and the carved-away areas will remain unpainted (the negative parts of the design).

3 If your design is very intricate, it helps to cut the carved motif out completely and stick it to a wooden or acrylic backing block. That way you have something solid to hold onto and the carved lino won't be damaged.

4 Once you think your lino stamp is ready, do a test print. You can apply your paint to the lino stamp with a sponge roller or by dabbing it on with a sponge. If there are printed areas where there shouldn't be, carve away the excess lino. Repeat this process until you are happy with the way the stamp is printing.

5 Print onto the fabric by placing your lino stamp, paint side down. Use a clean roller or brayer to roll firmly across the back of the stamp. Carefully peel the lino stamp off and reapply paint, ready to make the next print.

Lino stamps will last a long time if you wash them after use and store them flat.

foam stamps

Making printing blocks with foam sheets is an inexpensive and fun way to create stunning prints. You can easily buy foam sheets online or in the children's section of a stationery or art store.

Once you have cut the foam into the shape of your motif, you stick it onto a rigid backing—a wooden block, a wine coaster, or an acrylic block—to give you something to hold onto. The foam shape is the positive, raised part of the design that you coat with paint, while the block becomes the negative, unprinted area.

When printing certain designs, it helps to be able to see through the backing block to line up your prints. In that case, it's best to use an acrylic backing block.

how to use foam stamps

1 Transfer your design onto your sheet of foam. Take care when doing this as any small marks or indentations on the foam will show up in the finished print. On the other hand, you can use this to your advantage, scoring the foam deliberately to make a fine line or pushing the tip of a pencil in to make spots. However, don't crease the foam or make too many pencil lines if you want a good, clean print.

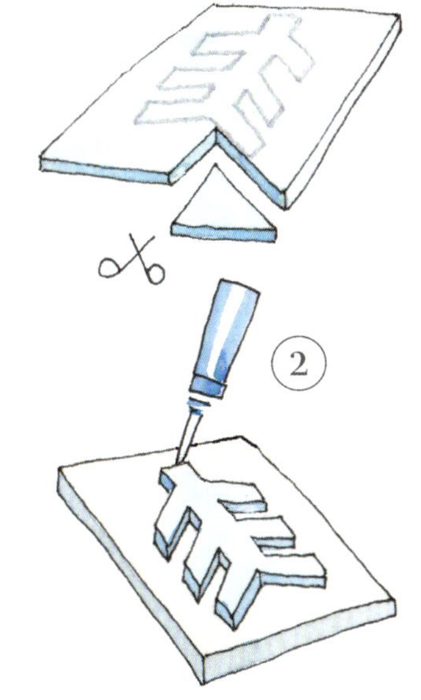

2 Cut out your foam shapes either with scissors or a craft knife and stick them to your backing block.

3 Foam sheets with a peel-off sticky backing are useful when cutting intricate designs. You can stick a whole piece of foam sheet to the block first, then cut out the design and peel away the unwanted foam. You can also use ready-cut foam shapes—the principle is the same.

4 Once your foam stamp is ready, use a sponge or a sponge roller to lightly coat the surface with paint. If you accidentally get any paint on the backing block, remove it with a clean cloth before you print. Place the stamp face down on the surface and press firmly and evenly on the back. Carefully remove the stamp and reapply the paint before the next print.

Foam stamps can be reused many times and will last well if washed carefully after use and if not stacked up together, as this will flatten the foam.

Extras you will need for printing with stamps: Erasers; lino sheets; foam sheets with a peel-off sticky backing; wooden or acrylic backing blocks; lino-cutting tools; roller or brayer

polystyrene tile

You may have memories of printing with polystyrene tiles at school. It is a simple technique where you push into the tile surface, creating areas where the paint cannot load and these will be the blank areas of your print.

how to print using a polystyrene tile

1 Use a pen or blunt pencil to make your marks.

2 Once your design is complete, load the paint onto the tile with a sponge roller and print by applying even pressure to the back of the tile, either with a clean brayer or your hands. This printing block is only good for a few projects because it is hard to keep the sheet undamaged. You could stick it to a firm backing if you wanted to preserve it for longer. Take care not to go through to the back when you are scoring your tile.

Extras you will need for printing with a polystyrene tile: Polystyrene tile, pen, scissors, sponge roller, roller/brayer

---

stencils and screen-printing

Stencils and screen-prints are forms of resist printing. In this type of printing, part of the design "resists" or blocks the paint and prevents it coming into contact with certain parts of the surface being printed. Stencils and screen-prints give a positive print so there is no need to worry about producing a design in reverse.

stencils

Stencils can be made from many different materials—paper, thin sheets of plastic, and masking tape are some examples. The stencil will "resist" the paint and prevent some areas from being printed.

Freezer paper is a plastic-coated kitchen paper that's great for stencils. If you place it shiny side down on fabric and iron over it, it will adhere to the fabric long enough for you to print. Alternatively, you can cut an ordinary paper stencil and use repositionable spray glue to hold it in place.

how to use a stencil

1 Draw your design onto the paper, leaving a wide border around the edge of the design. Cut out the design using a craft knife. If you are planning on a repeat design that is intended to cover a large area, you should cut several stencils the same as they will begin to clog up and degrade after a few uses.

2 Position your stencil on the fabric and sponge lightly or use a sponge roller to evenly coat the surface with fabric paint. Take care not to move the stencil as you apply the paint.

3 Leave to dry or use a hairdryer to speed up the drying, then remove the stencil. If you are working with a repeat design, reposition the stencil and sponge with paint again.

masking tape stencils

Using masking tape to create a stencil to "resist" the paint is one of the easiest ways to transform an object or a piece of fabric.

how to use masking tape stencils

1 Make sure that your fabric is ironed and flat or, if you are working with a painted surface, that it is clean and dry, with no flaking paint. Mark out your design with chalk if necessary, then apply the tape. Stick it down firmly, making sure the edges don't conceal any bubbles or gaps, or the paint will bleed underneath. Depending on your design, you can either mask off all the areas in one go, or you can mask one part at a time.

2 Apply paint to the fabric or surface. If you want to apply the paint in layers/stages, make sure it is thoroughly dry before moving on to masking for the next layer/stage. When you have finished, carefully remove all the tape and dry your paint completely before ironing the fabric.

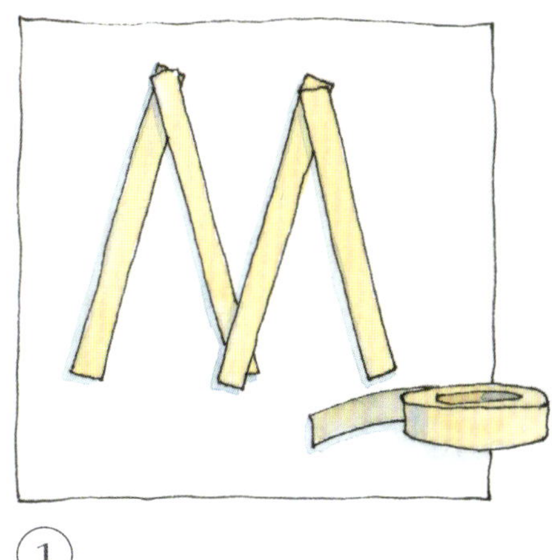

1

screen-printing

This is another type of stenciling. It involves using fine mesh fabric tightly stretched over a wooden or metal frame. You can attach a stencil to the screen to "resist" the paint, or use screen filler together with screen drawing fluid, or you can use screen filler on its own.

You can easily try various methods of screen-printing fabric at home without the need for expensive equipment. You can even make your own screen-printing frame (see page 15). The projects in this book are designed to give you the opportunity to try all the methods.

After using any of the screen-printing techniques, always allow the fabric paint to dry before ironing to heat-set it. Wash your screen immediately after use: never leave the paint to dry on the screen as it will ruin it.

how to screen-print using a stencil

1 Prepare your paper stencil by drawing your design in the center. The image should fit within the area of the mesh. Make sure you leave a border of 4in (10cm) of blank paper around the image. Cut it out with a craft knife.

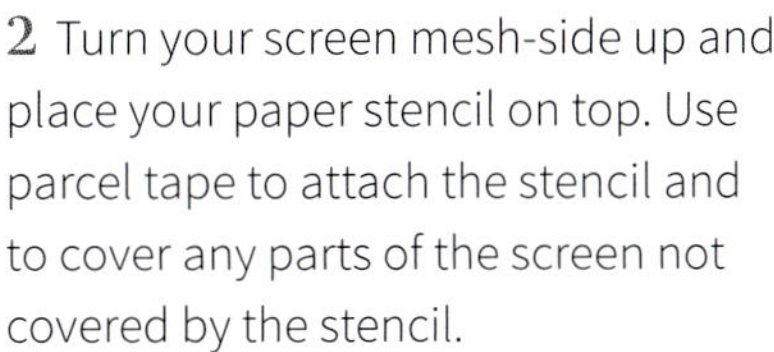

2 Turn your screen mesh-side up and place your paper stencil on top. Use parcel tape to attach the stencil and to cover any parts of the screen not covered by the stencil.

3 With your fabric on a flat surface, place the screen, stencil-side down, on top. Put a generous blob of paint on the screen above the image, then, using a squeegee the width of your screen, firmly and evenly drag the paint across the surface. Repeat twice more, then carefully lift up the screen and reposition it ready for the next print.

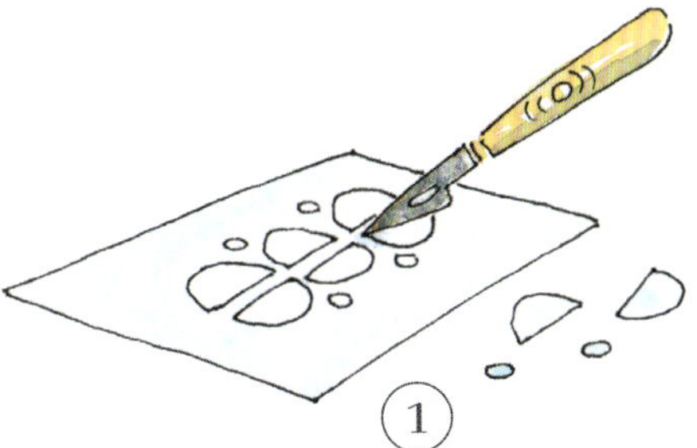

1

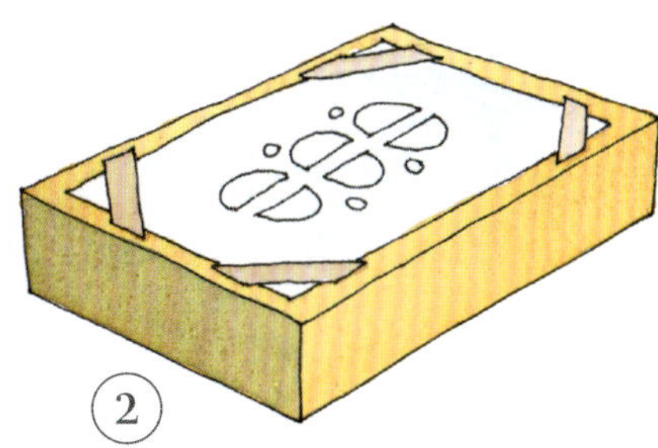

2

3

how to print using screen drawing fluid and screen filler

The following instructions apply when using any screen-printing frame, but here we show a home-made one (see page 15).

1 With the screen mesh-side down and a soft pencil—to avoid tearing the mesh—draw your motif onto the mesh. Leave a wide border around the edges.

2 Turn the screen mesh-side up and use a paintbrush and screen drawing fluid to paint over the penciled lines of the motif. You need to achieve a good solid line—if the line is too thin, the screen drawing fluid will wash out when you apply the screen filler, leaving parts of your design missing.

3 Leave the mesh to dry fully; use a hairdryer on a low heat if necessary.

4 Once the mesh is dry, coat your screen with screen filler. Do this with an old credit card or squeegee. Pour a blob of screen filler on the card and drag it across the screen, covering the surface with a thin, even coat. Take care not to overdo this or the drawing fluid will start to dissolve. Just drag the card quickly and smoothly once or twice across the screen.

5 You don't need to go right to the edges of the screen as these will be covered with parcel tape later on. Leave to dry, using a hairdryer on a low heat to speed things up.

6 Once the filler is completely dry, wash out the drawing fluid under running water. Allow the whole screen to dry, then prepare your screen for printing by covering the edges with parcel tape so no paint can get through to the fabric in areas where it shouldn't.

7 With the screen mesh-side down, put a generous blob of fabric paint on top and, using the credit card or squeegee, scrape the paint across the surface of the screen in one steady action.

8 Repeat a couple more times, then carefully lift up the screen and reposition it for the next print.

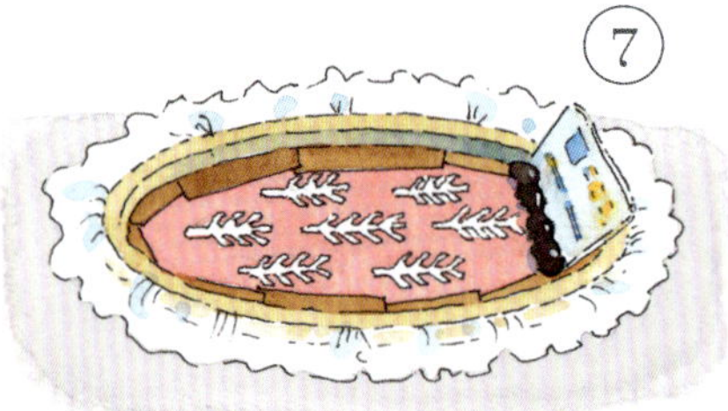

how to screen-print using screen filler on its own

1 With the screen mesh side down and a soft pencil—to avoid tearing the mesh—draw your motif onto the mesh. Leave a wide border around the edges of the motif.

2 Turn the screen mesh side up and paint around your motif with an even coat of screen filler. Once the filler is dry, it will act as a barrier—or "resist"—stopping any fabric paint seeping through onto the fabric in those areas. You don't need to paint right to the edges of the screen, just up to 2in (5cm) all around the motif.

3 Leave to dry fully; you can use a hairdryer to speed things. Once the filler is completely dry, cover the edges of the screen with parcel tape.

4 Lay your screen mesh-side down on the fabric. Using a credit card or squeegee, firmly and evenly drag the paint across the surface of the screen in one steady action.

5 Repeat a couple more times back and forth, then carefully lift up the screen and reposition it for the next print.

how to make your own screen-printing frame

1 You can make your own screen-printing frame using a two-part embroidery hoop and some very fine nylon fabric—either net curtain fabric or screen-printing fabric from a specialist supplier. Simply cut the fabric so it is about 4in (10cm) larger all around than the embroidery hoop. Place the mesh over the inner ring of the hoop, position the outer ring on top, and tighten the screw.

2 Work around the hoop, pulling the mesh tight as you go. Continue tightening the screw until the mesh is well stretched and securely held in place. Use parcel tape to cover the edges, leaving enough room for your print motif in the center.

Extras you will need for printing with stencils and screen-prints: Paper and repositionable spray glue or freezer paper; parcel tape; readymade screen-printing frame or an embroidery hoop and fine nylon mesh fabric; squeegee or old credit card; screen filler; screen drawing fluid; parcel tape; access to running water

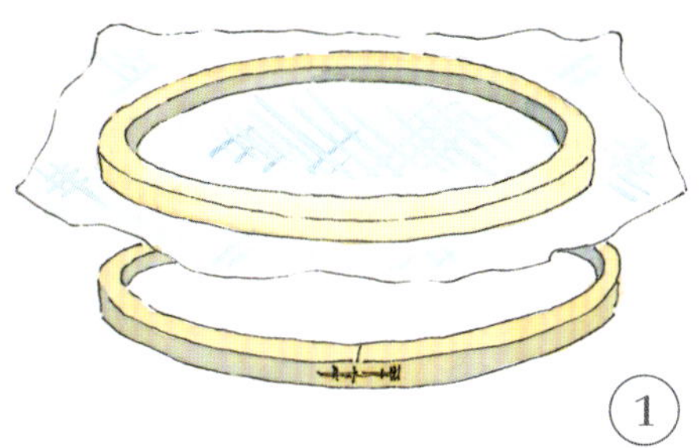

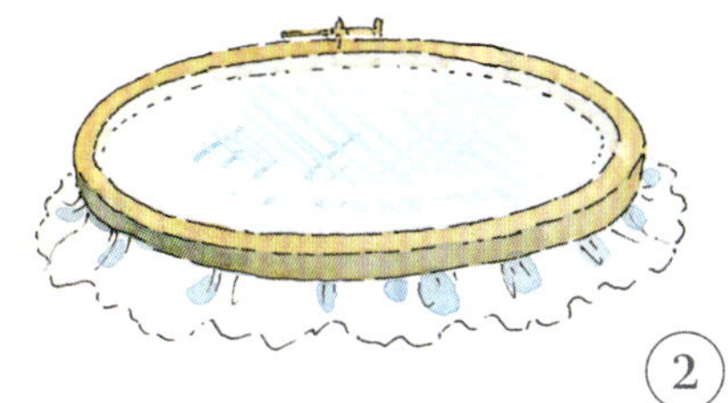

other printing methods

There are many other ways to make marks and transfer images to a surface. Here are the ones used in this book.

digital printing

There are different printing papers available that allow you to take images from the computer and transfer them to fabrics, ceramics, and other surfaces. Some of the projects in chapter 3 will let you try out these techniques—then you can use them with your own designs.

photo transfers

You can use drawing software on your computer to draw artworks, or use a photo-editing program to get photos ready to print out onto special inkjet photo transfer paper. Photo transfers will print back to front, so remember to reverse your photos before printing them out.

how to use photo transfers

1 Use your computer program to prepare your photo. Make it the required size and flip it so it is back to front. This is especially important if your photo has text on it. Failure to flip the photo will mean that your text will be a mirror image when it is printed.

2 Print your photo onto the right side of the photo transfer paper and cut it out, leaving a narrow border.

3 Place the paper, photo side down, on the fabric. Following the instructions that came with your paper, iron your transfer in place.

4 Peel away the backing to reveal the photo bonded to the fabric.

5 Do not iron directly on top of the bonded photo and take care when washing. Always follow the manufacturer's instructions to be extra sure.

ceramic transfers

Transferring images to ceramics and glass at home is easy when you use inkjet decal paper. You print out your image onto the special paper (there's no need to reverse the image), transfer it to your item, then bake it in the oven for a short time. The finish is not dishwasher-proof, so this technique isn't recommended for mugs and cups, but it is perfect for a vase or storage jar.

how to use ceramic transfers

1 Prepare the image on your computer and set the size and colors. Print the image onto the shiny (right) side of your inkjet decal paper, following the manufacturer's instructions.

2 Leave the ink to dry, then spray the paper with a few coats of clear varnish. The varnish will protect the ink from running when you place your transfer in water. Spray outside or in a well-ventilated area and leave to dry fully between coats.

3 Cut out your image, leaving a very narrow border around the edge. Place the transfer in a bowl of clean water and leave for 30 seconds or until you can feel the backing paper starting to slide off when you move it between your thumb and finger.

4 Leaving the backing in place, remove the transfer from the water and position it on your ceramic or glass item. Smooth the transfer down while gently sliding out the backing paper. Smooth the transfer with your finger to remove any air bubbles.

5 Once the transfer is in position, with no bubbles or creases, place the item in a preheated oven, following the manufacturer's instructions. The recommended temperature is usually 130°C/250°F/Gas ½. Once it has cooled, your item is ready to use.

Extras you will need for digital printing: Inkjet photo transfer paper; inkjet decal paper; inkjet printer; clear spray varnish

leaf printing

This is so simple and yet it can lead to designs you'd never expect.

how to leaf print

1 Roller or apply the paint onto the back of a leaf and place it on the fabric.

2 Place the leaf paint-side down onto the fabric. Use a clean roller to press, and carefully peel off the leaf. Depending on how delicate the leaf is you can get a few prints from one leaf. Let the garden inspire you and try out different things.

Extras you will need for printing with leaves: Leaves, sponge roller or paint brush, clean roller/brayer

top printing tips

preparation

- For every technique involving printing fabric you will need a large flat surface for printing that's protected from the fabric paints with old newspaper, a plastic tablecloth, cut-up plastic refuse sacks, or an old shower curtain. Set up your working space so the paints and sponges are well away from the fabric, to prevent any accidents.
- Always iron your fabric before printing so it lies flat and smooth.
- Do a test print! Always—no matter how confident you are—try out your print on some scrap fabric first, it will help you to get your final project perfect first time.
- If a print design is complicated—or if it is a geometric design that needs to be straight or aligned—it's a great idea to mark where you want your pattern to be on the fabric before you start to print. You can do this with a pencil or chalk.
- If your design calls for simple stripes, then you could use masking tape to mask off the areas you don't want to print.

printing

- It's always best to use a small sponge or brush to apply the paint to potato prints to get a smoother covering.
- Use baby wipes or a clean wet rag to clean off the edges of printing blocks after loading with paint. This will help to prevent many imperfections.
- Don't allow fabric paint to dry on your printing block as it will ruin it and it won't be usable again.
- When working with text always remember to reverse your design!

layering

- Try layering a few different printing techniques together. For example, you could use large stencils combined with rubber stamps.
- Always make sure the paint is dry in between layers or it will bleed and smudge—and always print your background first, if you have one. A hairdryer is a useful addition to your working space to dry layers between prints.

setting

- Always set your printed fabric by ironing with a hot iron; this will make it waterproof and give a clean, crisp finish.

CHAPTER 1

stamps

honeycomb bunting

Bunting is great for brightening up a space. This bee-themed bunting is sure to bring some sunshine into your home. You can make your bunting as long as you need by adding more triangles.

skill level: ●

printing technique
foam stamp (see page 11)

materials

Bee and hexagon print motifs on page 115

Main fabric
Approx. 28 x 12in (70 x 30cm)

Lining fabric
Approx. 28 x 12in (70 x 30cm)

Pencil, ruler
Bias binding: 99in (2.5m)

printing tools

Foam sheets
Scissors
Wooden or acrylic backing block
Glue
Sponge or sponge roller
Fabric paint in three colors

1 Iron your fabrics and cut them to size. Draw your triangles on the fabrics using a pencil and a ruler. The triangles in this design are 8in (22cm) along the top edge and 8in (22cm) from the center of the top edge to the point. To fit in as many triangles as possible, rotate every other triangle through 180 degrees, but leave a 1in (25mm) gap in between your triangles.

2 This project was created using three different shades of orange fabric paint and three foam-sheet printing blocks—one for printing the bee, one for the hexagon outlines, and one for the solid hexagons. Prepare your foam stamps as described on page 11, using the bee and hexagon motifs on page 115. Load each stamp with one of the fabric paints using a sponge, and build up your design on the main fabric triangles. Practice first on a scrap of fabric until you are confident you can achieve a clean, clear print.

3 You can make a repeated pattern with your hexagons or just place them randomly on the triangles. Print at least 2 triangles with each of your blocks so you have an even number of different triangles for your bunting. Your motifs can overlap the edges of the triangles.

4 When you are happy with your design, iron the fabric to set the paint, then cut out all your printed triangles and your lining triangles.

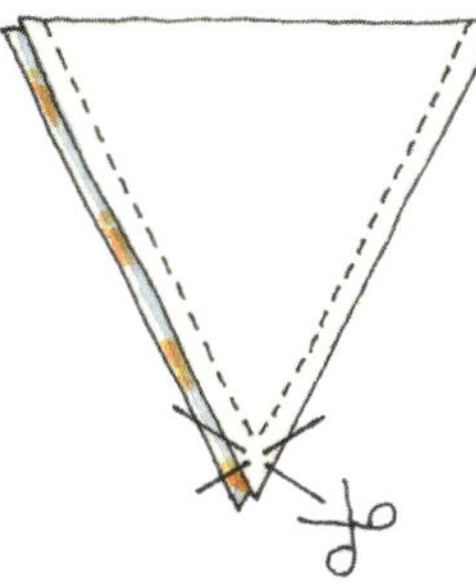

5 Place a printed triangle and a lining triangle right sides together. Using a ⅜in (1cm) seam allowance (see page 110), sew around the two long sides, then trim away the point, taking care not to cut through the stitching. Turn the triangle right-side out and press. Repeat with all your triangles.

6 To join your triangles together to make a strip of bunting, press your bias binding in half all along its length.

7 Leaving the first 10in (25cm) of bias binding clear, place the unstitched side of your first triangle in between the folded binding. Pin in place. Sew along the edge of the bias binding to keep the triangle in place, then continue adding all the triangles in the same way, leaving a 3in (8cm) gap between each one. Leave 10in (25cm) at the other end of the binding for hanging.

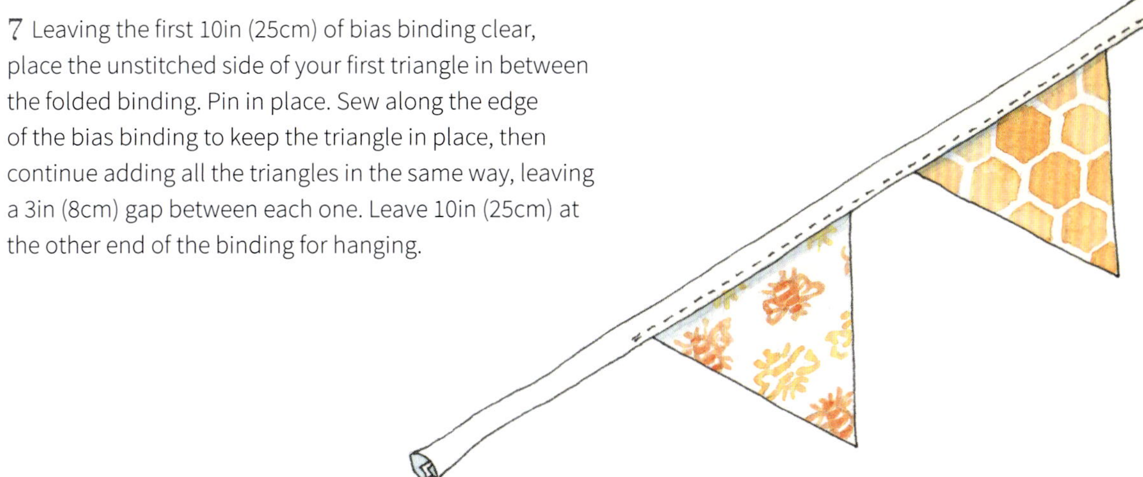

tea cozy

A timeless classic, this project shows you how to make your own quilted tea cozy to keep a refreshing pot of tea warm for ages. This tea cozy will fit a teapot that is 6in (15cm) tall and 12in (30cm) wide, but you can adapt it to fit your own teapot by measuring your teapot and making the template larger or smaller.

skill level ●●●

printing technique

foam stamp (see page 11)

materials

Teapot and teacup print motifs on page 115

Fabric template on page 122

Main fabric

Panel 1: cut two, 10 x 12in (25 x 30cm)

Panel 2: cut two, 5 x 12in (12 x 30cm)

Panel 3: cut two, 5 x 12in (12 x 30cm)

Teabag tag: cut two, 2½ x 2½in (6 x 6cm)

Lining fabric

Cut two, 17¾ x 12in (45 x 30cm)

Batting (wadding)

Cut two, 17¾ x 12in (45 x 30cm)

Short length of ribbon

Needle, pins, matching thread

printing tools

Foam sheets

Scissors

Wooden or acrylic backing block

Glue

Pencil eraser

Fabric paint

Sponge or sponge roller

1 This tea cozy is made up of three printed panels joined together to make one piece of fabric for each side of the tea cozy. Prepare your foam stamps as described on page 11, using the teapot and teacup motifs on page 115.

2 Iron your fabrics and cut them to size, making them a little larger than the fabric template requires. Lay the fabrics on a flat surface for printing.

3 Load your teapot stamp with fabric paint using a sponge and apply to each of the two large panels of fabric, one for each side of the cozy. Practice first on a scrap of fabric until you are confident you can achieve a clean, clear print.

4 Now load a pencil eraser with fabric paint using a sponge, then use this to build up the spots around the teapots. You might like to leave some areas of fabric unprinted. Build up the spots in the same way on both sets of the smaller panels of fabric.

5 To make the little teabag tag, cut the fabric to the size required and print a teacup centrally on each piece. Iron all your printed fabrics to set the paint.

6 Now you must join the three panels of printed fabric together for each side of the cozy. Join one panel to the next, right side to right side and sew them together leaving a ½in (1cm) seam allowance (see page 110). Repeat until you have two lots of three panels.

7 Press the seams open (see page 110) and topstitch (see page 112) neatly down both sides of each seam, as a decorative detail.

8 Now you are going to use the fabric template on page 122 to cut each set of panels into the shape of the tea cozy. Use the template to shape your two pieces of lining fabric and the two pieces of batting as well.

9 Quilting the lining fabric will make the tea cozy hold the heat better. Do this by laying a piece of batting on the wrong side of each piece of lining fabric, then sew the two together using criss-crossed diagonal lines of stitching spaced approximately 2in (5cm) apart.

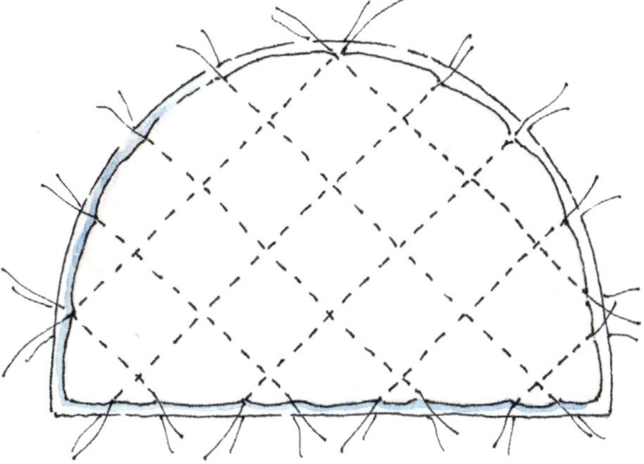

10 You now have two quilted pieces of lining. With right side to right side and leaving a ½in (1cm) seam allowance, sew them together around the curved edge to make a quilted lining pouch.

DESIGN TIP

To give this project a twist, you can print two different types of fabric and join them before cutting out the shape of the tea cozy.

11 You now need to make the little teabag tag. Lay your two pieces of printed teabag fabric with right sides together, making sure the teacup print is the same way up on each side. Pin the ends of your ribbon in between at the center top (the rim of the printed teacup), with the loop facing inward.

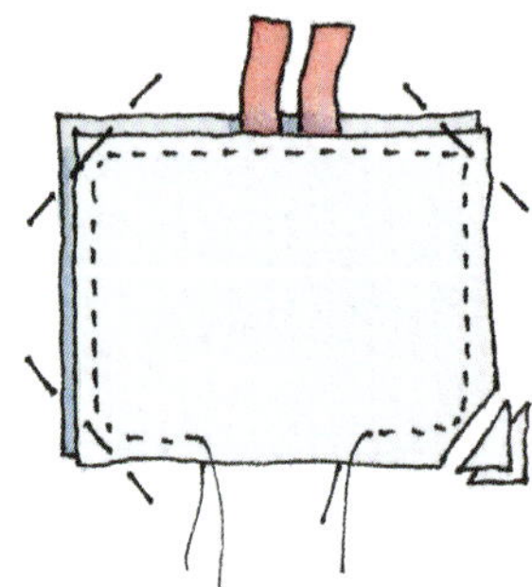

12 Leaving a ½in (1cm) seam allowance, sew around all four sides of the tag. Leave a small opening for turning. Trim the corners (see page 112), turn right side out, and press. Pin the opening closed and sew a neat line of topstitches all around the edge.

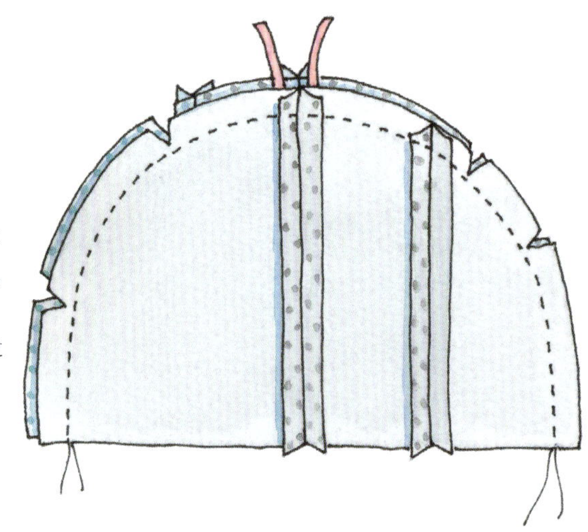

13 Now line up the two shaped pieces of printed fabric with right sides together and pin the ribbon ends of your teabag tag in between the two layers at the center top. Leaving a ½in (1cm) seam allowance, sew around the curved edge, then clip the curves, taking care not to cut through the stitches. Turn right side out and press.

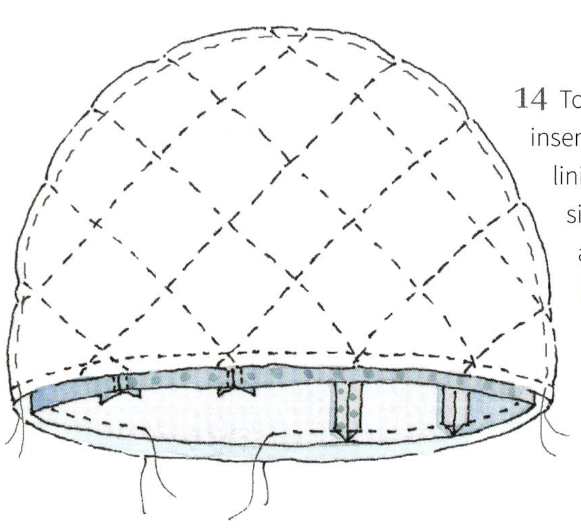

14 To construct your tea cozy, insert the printed fabric into the lining fabric pouch with right sides together. Pin together all around the bottom edge. Leaving a ½in (1cm) seam allowance, sew around the bottom edge, leaving a small opening for turning.

15 Turn to the right side through the opening, push the lining inside, and hand-sew the opening closed to finish your tea cozy.

quilted oven glove

This oven glove not only gives practical protection when you're taking your baking out of the oven, but is a stylish addition to any kitchen. You could use colors that match your decor or add a bright splash of contrast color if you prefer.

skill level: ●●

printing technique

fruit and vegetable print (see page 9) and eraser stamp (see page 10)

materials

Leaf and stem print motifs on page 115

Fabric template on page 124

Main fabric

Front and back: cut two, 8 x 13in (20 x 33cm)

Hanging loop: 4 x 2in (10 x 5cm)

Lining fabric

Cut two, 8 x 13in (20 x 33cm)

Thermal batting (wadding)

Cut two, 8 x 13in (20 x 33cm)

Matching thread

printing tools

2 potatoes

Kitchen knife

Pencil eraser

Fabric paint in 3 colors

Sponge

1 Carve your potatoes, as described on page 9, using the pairs of leaves and stems motifs on page 115. The berries are added afterward, using a pencil eraser as a stamp. Practice first on a scrap of fabric until you are confident you can achieve a clean, clear print.

2 Iron your fabric, cut it to size, and lay it on a flat surface ready for printing. First load the leaf stamp with fabric paint using a sponge.

3 Start at the bottom left-hand corner of the fabric and print the pairs of leaves in rows, staggering each row like a brick pattern. Then load the stems stamp with fabric paint in another color and add those between each pair of leaves. Finally load the pencil eraser with fabric paint in the third color to add the berries to the stems. Don't forget to print the piece of fabric for your hanging loop, too.

4 When you are happy with your finished design, iron the fabric to set the paint.

5 Cut out your printed fabric, lining, and batting using the fabric template on page 124. Trim the batting so it is ½in (1cm) smaller all around than the printed fabric.

6 Now you are going to pad the printed fabric for heat protection. Do this by laying a piece of batting on the wrong side of each piece of the printed fabric. Pin or baste (tack) the batting in place so it won't move about.

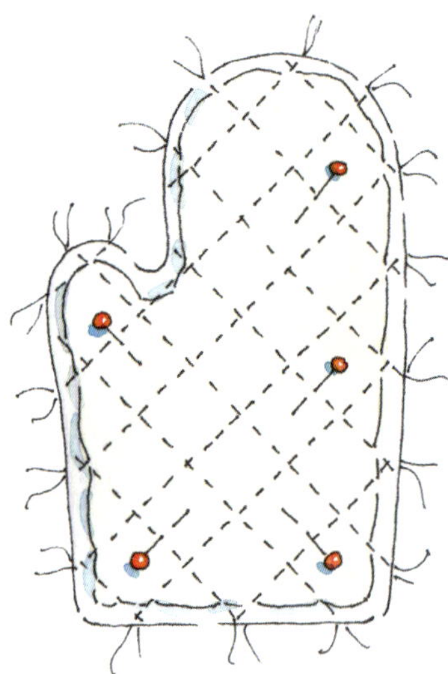

7 Working on the right side of the printed fabric, machine-sew the two together using criss-crossed diagonal lines of stitching spaced approximately 1in (3cm) apart.

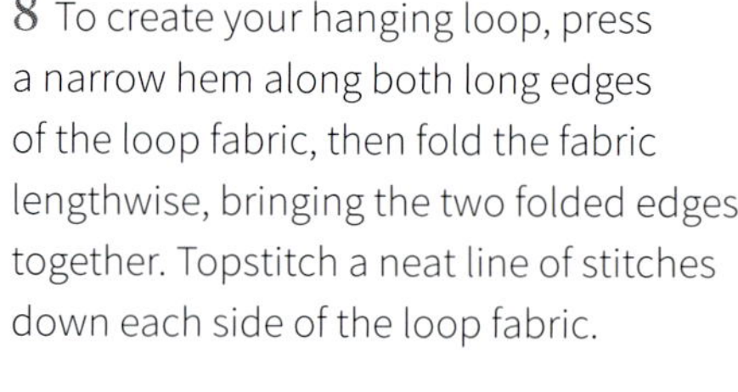

8 To create your hanging loop, press a narrow hem along both long edges of the loop fabric, then fold the fabric lengthwise, bringing the two folded edges together. Topstitch a neat line of stitches down each side of the loop fabric.

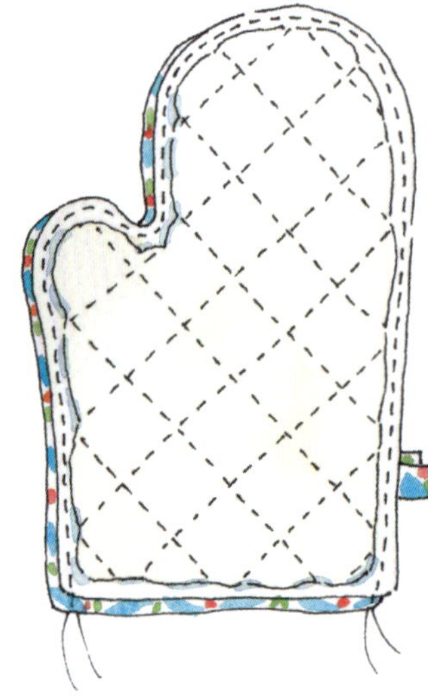

9 Place the two quilted pieces of fabric right sides together. Tuck the hanging loop between them, facing inward. Leaving a ½in (1cm) seam allowance (see page 110), sew all around the edge, making sure to avoid catching the batting in your stitches, as this will make the seam too bulky. Trim more batting away if necessary.

10 Clip the curves and especially round the thumb, taking care not to cut through the stitches (see page 112). Leave the glove inside out.

11 Now you are going to make up your lining. Place the two pieces of lining right sides together. Leaving a ½in (1cm) seam allowance, sew all around the edge. Clip the curves and the thumb, being careful not to cut through the stitches. Turn to the right side.

12 Insert the lining into the quilted glove so the right sides of both are facing. Line up the bottom edges, then sew around the bottom edge, leaving a ½in (1cm) seam allowance. Leave a 4in (10cm) opening. Pull the glove to the right side through the opening. Push all the curves and the thumb out fully. Tuck the lining back inside the glove, but leave a ½in (1cm) border of lining around the glove opening. Pin the opening closed. You will sew it closed in the next step.

13 Tuck your glove over the free arm of your sewing machine and sew a ½in (1cm) seam along the edge of the lining.

PRINTING TIPS

This print is made up of three elements layered one on top of the other. You start by printing the pairs of big leaves, then everything else will fit in. Practice your placement on scrap fabric first till you are confident. If you are really aiming at perfection, mark your fabric with chalk lines and follow these when you print.

wall printing

Printing directly onto a wall is a great way to transform any space. You can be as ambitious or as conservative as you like—print the whole wall or just a small area.

skill level: ●

printing technique

foam stamp (see page 11)

materials

Insect print motifs on page 115

A wall!

printing tools

Foam sheets

Craft knife

Scissors

Wooden or acrylic backing blocks

Glue

Chalk or masking tape (optional)

Acrylic paint in a variety of colors

Sponge

Paintbrush (optional)

1 Make sure the wall you are going to print on is clean, dry, and as smooth as possible. A wall painted with matt emulsion is best. Gloss paint is slippery to work on and woodchip and bare brick will be very tricky and will give poor results.

2 If you need to paint the wall before you start, make sure to leave 24 hours before you print so the paint is completely dry.

3 Prepare your foam stamps as described on page 11, using the three insect motifs on page 115.

4 Plan out your printing pattern before you begin. You can do this by eye or by measuring. Use chalk or little strips of masking tape to mark the positions of each motif. If you are covering a large surface, stand back and check that the placement is right.

5 Once you are happy with your design, you can begin to print. Load the stamp with paint using a sponge. Take care not to use too much paint or the stamp will slip and slide on the wall and you won't get a perfect print. If at all possible, do a test print somewhere on the wall that won't be visible (for example, behind a mirror, or a framed picture). This will help you to see how it feels to print on a wall.

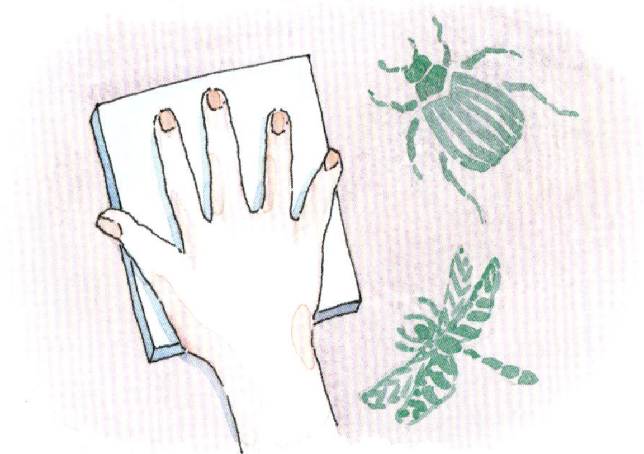

6 Print your motifs one at a time, working first with one color across the whole area, then changing colors to build up the rest of the design. Here, some of the prints have been overlaid with a second color to give the design more definition. To do the same, simply wait for the first color to dry, then load your stamp with your second color and carefully line up and print over the top. This is where acrylic backing blocks really help because you can see exactly where your print is going.

7 Once you have printed all your motifs, allow them to dry naturally. Acrylic paint is as durable as wall paint and does not need heat-setting or sealing with varnish.

PRINTING TIPS

Be extra-careful that the stamp doesn't slip when printing on the wall. Hold on to it well. You can touch up your prints with a small paintbrush to cover up any imperfections.

children's backpack

This useful little backpack is great for a day at the beach, an after-school activity, or carrying school sports kit. The print design used here is a nautical scene built up with three different pictorial elements.

skill level ●●●

printing technique
lino (see page 10)

materials

Boat, seagull, and wave print motifs on page 117

Main fabric

Main panel: cut two, 14 x 16½in (35 x 42cm)

Cord tabs: cut two, 2 x 3in (5 x 8cm)

Matching thread

Cord, approx. 79in (2m)

printing tools

Lino sheet

Lino cutters

Fabric paint

Sponge roller

1 Prepare your lino as described on page 10. Cut out your fabric and press it ready to print. Apply the print. Once your print is dry, iron your fabric at a high temperature to set the fabric paint.

2 To make the tabs for the cord to be threaded through, take your strips of fabric, fold in half, then press a ⅜in (1cm) hem on both edges. Fold in the middle so that the edges meet up and topstitch (see page 112) down both edges to finish. Make up two tabs.

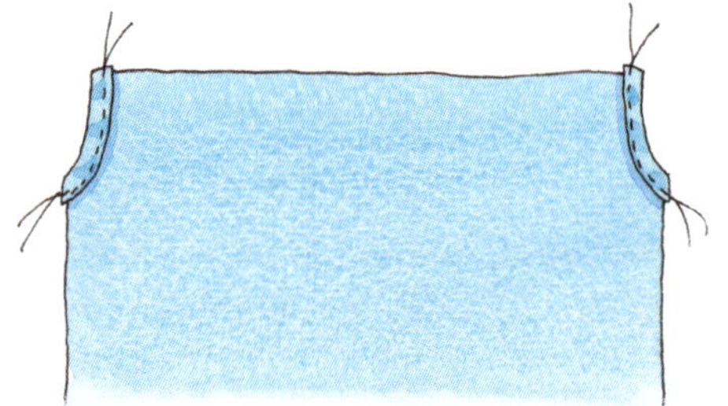

3 Prepare the top edges of the bag to make neat openings for the cord handles. Make a snip approximately ⅜in (1cm) into the side edges, 2in (5cm) down from the top edge on both sides. Fold over, press, and sew a ⅜in (1cm) seam on both sides.

4 To make the channel through which the cord handles will be threaded, fold over and press a ⅜in (1cm) hem along the whole top edge, and then fold again, press, and sew a ⅜in (2cm) hem creating a channel along the top edge. Do this on both pieces of fabric.

5 French seams (see page 111) are used to make up the bag. Take the two main pieces of fabric and place them wrong sides together. Pin the cord tabs that you made in step 2, 2in (5cm) up from the bottom of the bag, facing inward toward the center of the bag and sew a ⅜in (1cm) seam around the two sides and bottom.

6 Trim the seam edges down so that they are as narrow as you can make them without compromising the stitches. Turn inside out and press the seams. Sew another ⅜in (1cm) seam down the sides enclosing all the raw edges inside and securing the tabs on each side. Turn right side out and press.

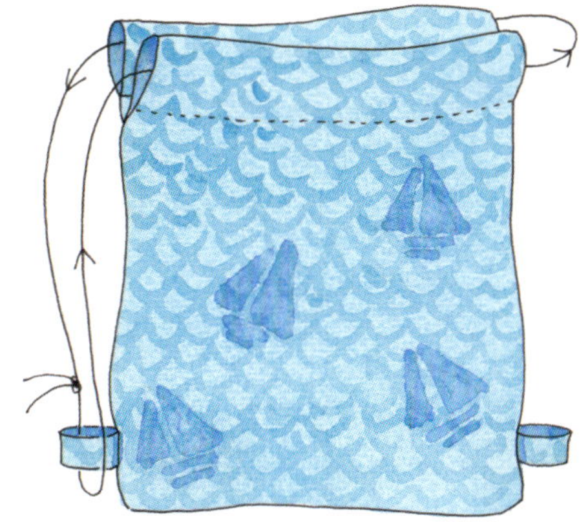

7 To thread the handle cord to the bag, attach a safety pin to one end of the cord to help you to guide it through the channels. Start by threading one end of the cord around the top of the bag and out of the same side hole it went into. Run the cord right down to the tab at the bottom and thread one end through the tab, then tie the two ends together. Repeat on the other side of the bag in the same way. Now, when you pull the handles they will open and close the bag top.

leafy lampshade

Lampshade kits are readily available and come in all shapes and sizes. This project is for a small drum lampshade—a great first lampshade project that will brighten up any room. It's not as tricky as you may think. Alternatively, you could revamp an old lampshade by re-covering it with your newly printed fabric.

skill level ●●

printing technique

foam stamp (see page 11)

materials

Leaf print motifs on page 116

Lampshade kit

Fabric (see lampshade kit for size required)

Scissors

Stiff card (optional)

printing tools

Foam sheets

Scissors

Wooden or acrylic backing block

Glue

Fabric paint in three colors

Sponge

1 Before you begin, check the size of fabric required for your kit, if using. Iron your fabric and cut it out, making it slightly larger than the required size. Lay it on a flat surface ready for printing.

2 Prepare your stems of leaves foam stamps as described on page 11, using the motifs on page 116.

3 Load each stamp with one of the fabric paints using a sponge, and build up your design on the fabric by overlapping the leaves. Practice first on a scrap of fabric until you are confident you can achieve a clean, clear print.

4 When you are happy with your design, iron the fabric to set the paint. You're now ready to begin assembling your lampshade.

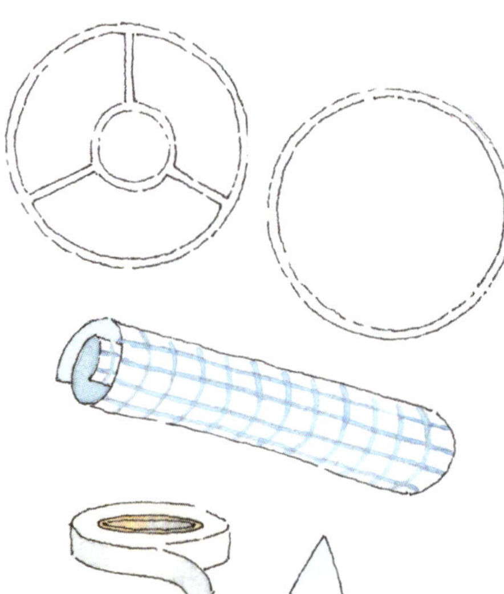

5 If you are using a lampshade kit, make sure you familiarize yourself with the accompanying instructions. Kits come with 2 metal rings to form the top and bottom of the lamp, a roll of heat-resistant plastic with a peel-off sticky backing for reinforcing your fabric, double-sided tape to stick the rings to the fabric, and a finishing tool for tucking away the raw edges.

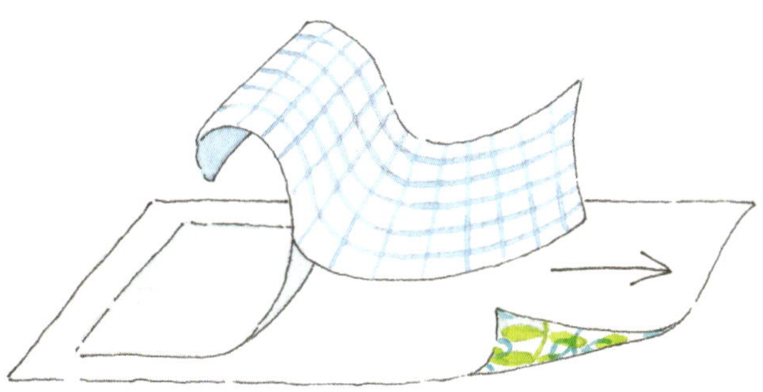

6 Lay your fabric out, printed side down. Peel off the first 4in (10cm) of the backing from the plastic. Starting at one end of your fabric and peeling off the backing gradually, stick the plastic to the fabric, making sure you smooth out the plastic and fabric as you go. Trim your fabric to the recommended size according to the kit instructions.

7 Next, prepare your metal lampshade rings by attaching the double-sided tape all the way around both rings. Remove the backing tape on both rings and place them on either edge of your fabric at one end. Make sure the light fitting is pointing toward the inside of your lamp and is on the correct side, depending on how you intend to use the lampshade. If it is going to be for a pendant light, the fitting will need to be at the top of the lamp but if you are going to use it on a lamp base, it will need to be at the bottom. Slowly roll both rings at once along the edges of the fabric to stick the fabric to the rings.

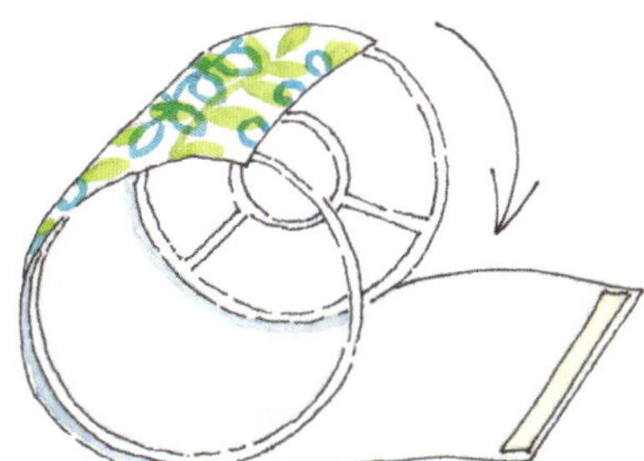

8 Just before you get to the end, add a strip of double-sided tape along the final edge of the fabric. Remove the backing paper, then continue rolling the rings to stick the final edge of the fabric in place.

9 Fold the excess fabric at the top and bottom of the lampshade over the metal rings. Use the finishing tool provided in the kit or pieces of stiff card to tuck away any raw edges—and you're done.

PRINTING TIPS

This design is made up of a simple stem of leaves, one in solid color and the other in outline. Layering the two together in a random way and using different shades of paint will give you an interesting print with lots of depth.

doorstop cube

This cube doorstop is a great alternative to a traditional, solid doorstop. It is nice and soft but is filled with sand or rice to add weight and hold the door in place.

skill level ●●

printing technique

lino print (see page 10)

materials

Geometric print motif on page 116

Main fabric

Main panels: cut one, 8 x 51in (20 x 130cm)

Handle: cut two, 2 x 8in (5 x 20cm)

Strong plastic bag

Sand or rice, for filling

Scissors, pins, needle, matching thread

printing tools

Lino sheet

Lino cutter

Craft knife

Fabric paint in 3 colors

Sponge

Sponge or sponge roller

1 Prepare your lino stamp as described on page 10, using the motif on page 116. To print, load the stamp with fabric paint using a sponge or a sponge roller. Practice first on a scrap of fabric until you are confident you can achieve a clean, clear print that is correctly lined up.

2 Iron your fabric, cut it to size, and lay it on a flat surface ready for printing. Build up your design by printing in vertical rows. The top of each print should touch the bottom of the last print. After printing one row, rotate the lino stamp 180 degrees for the next row. Make sure the sides of the prints in the second row are touching the sides of the prints in the first row. You can change your colors when you like.

3 When you are happy with your finished design, iron the fabric to set the paint.

4 Now you must cut the strip into six 7 x 7in (18 x 18cm) squares. You will create the doorstop by sewing the squares together to form a cube. Choose one of your squares as the bottom of your doorstop. With right sides together, pin and sew four side panels around each side of the first square. Leave a ½in (1cm) seam allowance (see page 110) and start and end each seam ½in (1cm) from the corner. Lift up the four panels and, still with the wrong sides of the fabric facing you, sew them together to make a cube. You will sew the final square onto the top of the cube in step 6.

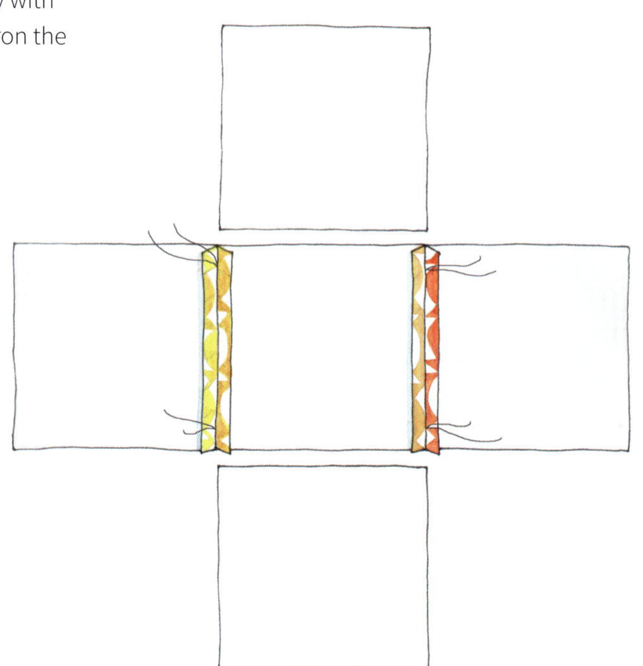

5 Next you need to make up your handle. With right side to right side, sew the two handle pieces together with a ½in (1cm) seam down both edges. Turn to the right side and press to get nice crisp edges. Topstitch (see page 112) a neat line of stitches close to both edges.

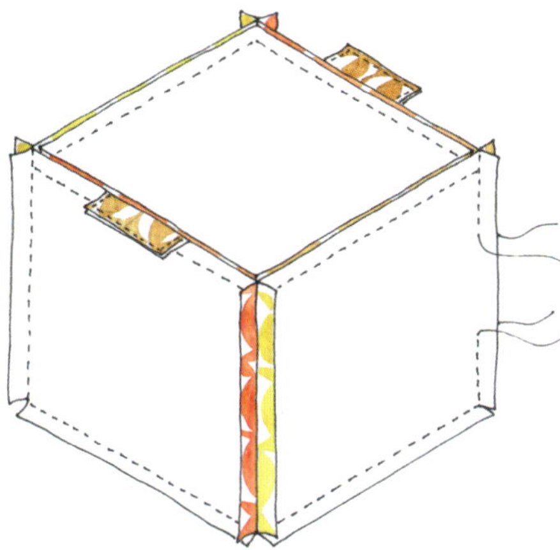

6 Now you need to attach the top panel and the handle at the same time. Pin the handle to the center of the top panel then, with right sides together, pin the sides of the top panel to the four side panels, sandwiching the ends of the handle between the layers. Sew around the sides of the top panel, leaving a ½in (1cm) seam allowance.

7 Turn the doorstop to the right side through the opening, then push out the corners from the inside to make sure the cube has a good shape.

8 Line the cube with a strong plastic bag so your filling doesn't escape through the seams, then use a funnel to fill the cube with sand or rice until the doorstop is firm.

9 Tie a tight knot in the plastic bag and tuck it inside the cube. Hand-sew the opening closed and your doorstop is ready to use.

PRINTING TIPS

This motif is printed in vertical rows. Rotate the lino stamp 180 degrees every other row to build up the pattern. This design has a random pattern but you could use one color for each row.

toiletry bag

This is a simple flat-bottomed, zippered bag, but it's made a little taller, so there's plenty of room, and lined with waterproof fabric. The print is a repeated rose, which is a great introduction to layered printing. It's made up of three layers of color: a block color, the outline, and the leaf detail.

skill level ●●

printing technique

foam stamps (see page 11)

materials

Rose and leaf print motifs on page 116

Main fabric

Main panel: cut two, 11in (28cm) square

Handle strip: cut one, 10 x 1½in (25 x 4cm)

Waterproof lining fabric

Cut two, 11in (28cm) square

Matching zipper: 8in (20cm)

Matching thread

printing tools

Craft foam sheets

Three wood or acrylic blocks, 3in (8cm) square

Glue

Sharp knife

Fabric paint

Sponge roller

1 Prepare your foam sheets as described on page 11. Cut out your main fabric pieces larger than the pattern states and iron them. Apply the print, allowing each layer to dry before you start the next. Once the fabric is completely dry, iron it to set the fabric paint.

2 Cut out the fabric pieces accurately—10in (25cm) along the bottom, 10in (25cm) tall, and then taper both sides until the top measures just 8in (20cm). Make up the handle—fold and press a ⅜in (1cm) hem on both sides of the handle strip, fold in half so that the sides meet, and topstitch (over sew) seams down both sides.

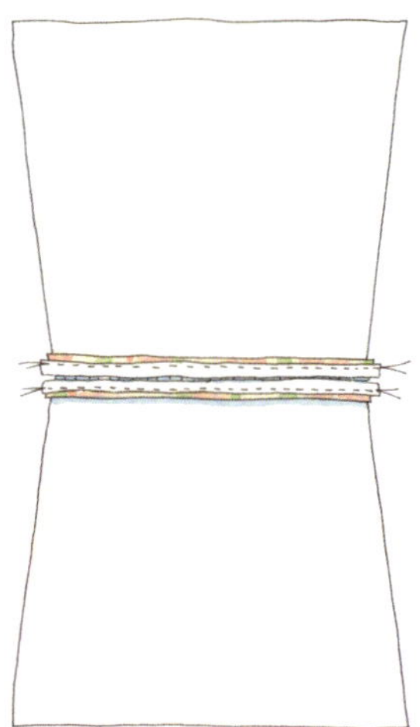

3 Attach your zipper foot to your machine, place the zipper face down along the top edge of one side of the main fabric and sew in place along the edge, right sides facing (see page 113). Line up the zipper with the top edge of the other side of main fabric and sew in place in the same way.

4 To attach the lining to the zipper, repeat the same process, but on the other side of the zipper. Lay your main fabric flat on its wrong side, with the zipper in the center, and press. Place one piece of lining fabric over the top and match its position to the turned over edge of the main fabric, covering the zipper. Pin and sew a neat seam following the same line of stitches as used to secure the main fabric, repeat on the other side. Lay out flat and press.

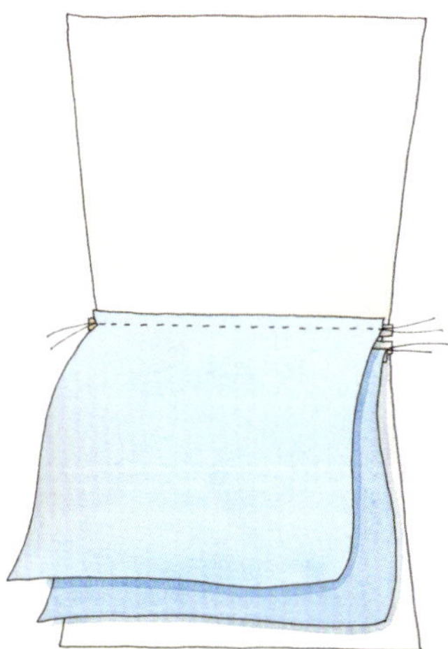

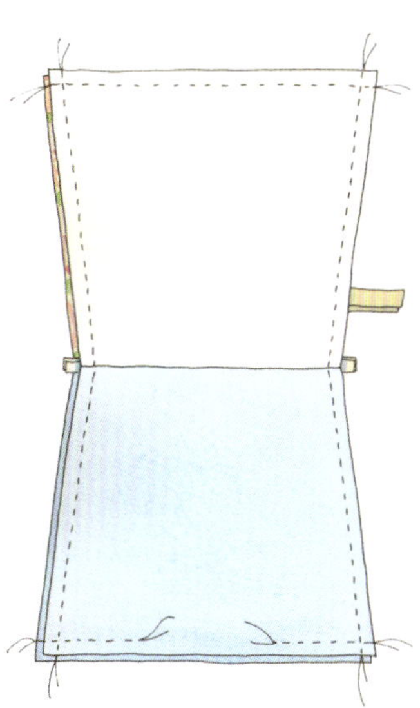

5 Open out the fabric, matching the lining pieces and the main fabric pieces right sides together. Pin the handle in place between the main fabric pieces, facing inward. With the zipper hidden in the center and the right sides of the fabric pieces together, sew a ⅜in (1cm) seam all around the outer edges leaving a 2in (5cm) gap at the base of the lining and capturing the handle in the seam.

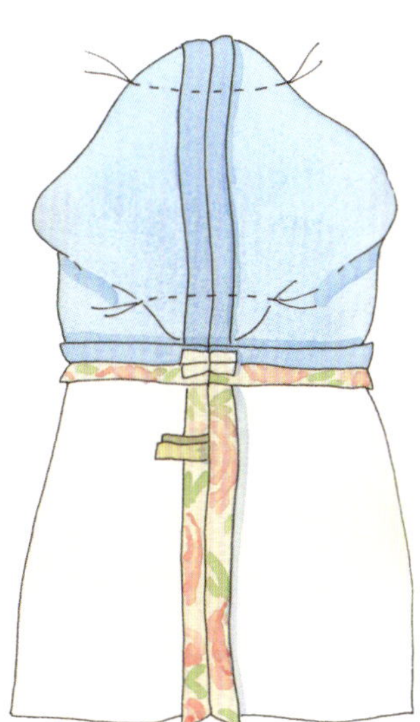

6 On the lining fabric piece, fold the fabric so that the bottom of the bag is flattened, the seam is in the center, and two protruding corner triangles are created. Press flat and sew a diagonal closing seam 1½in (4cm) in from each corner. Repeat this on the main fabric. Trim the corners off (see page 112).

7 Pull the bag through the opening in the lining fabric, turn it right side out, and press the top edge away from the zipper. Sew the opening in the lining closed.

envelope clutch

This stylish clutch is perfect for an evening out, a wedding, or a glamorous event. It's a practical size to hold all your essentials, and has an eye-catching design. This is an easy pattern to make up as it uses only a rectangle and a triangle of fabric.

skill level: ●●

printing technique
lino (see page 10)

materials

Feather motifs on page 116

Main fabric

Main piece: cut one, 17½ x 12½in (44 x 32cm)

Flap piece: cut one, 12½ x 9½in (32 x 24cm)

Lining fabric

Main piece: cut one, 17½ x 12½in (44 x 32cm)

Flap piece: cut one, 12½ x 9½in (32 x 24cm)

Iron-on interfacing

Main piece: cut one, 17½ x 12½in (44 x 32cm)

Flap piece: cut one, 12½ x 9½in (32 x 24cm)

Magnetic bag clasp

Matching thread

printing tools

Lino sheet

Lino cutters

Fabric paint

Sponge roller

1 Prepare your lino blocks as described on page 10. Then, cut out the pieces of your main fabric slightly larger than the measurements given in the materials list, mark where you want the print in chalk or pencil, and print your design onto the fabric. Once it's dry, iron it to set the fabric paint. Now you can accurately cut out your pattern pieces in all fabrics.

2 On both the main and the lining fabrics, working on the wrong side, find and mark the center of the main piece with a line of chalk or pencil. Measure 2½in (6cm) from the top edge on both long sides and mark. Draw a connecting, diagonal line from the side mark to the center at the end and cut on this line. Iron the interfacing onto all the main fabric pieces.

3 To attach the magnetic clasp (see page 114), work first with the top part of the clasp (the thinner part). On the lining fabric flap piece, iron on a small piece of interfacing, to cover and strengthen the triangle point, to about 4in (10cm) high. Measure up 2½in (6cm) from the point and mark, measure in 2in (5cm) from both sides to meet your first measurement and mark. On the right side of the fabric, cut two small slits next to the mark and push the fixing arms of the clasp through the fabric. On the wrong side of the fabric, fold the fixing arms over each other to secure in place.

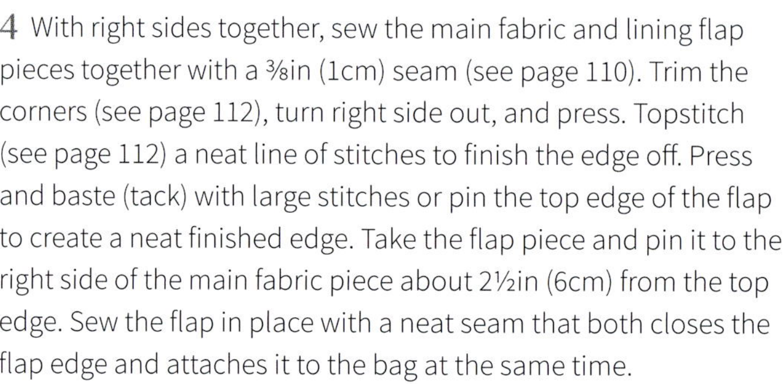

4 With right sides together, sew the main fabric and lining flap pieces together with a ⅜in (1cm) seam (see page 110). Trim the corners (see page 112), turn right side out, and press. Topstitch (see page 112) a neat line of stitches to finish the edge off. Press and baste (tack) with large stitches or pin the top edge of the flap to create a neat finished edge. Take the flap piece and pin it to the right side of the main fabric piece about 2½in (6cm) from the top edge. Sew the flap in place with a neat seam that both closes the flap edge and attaches it to the bag at the same time.

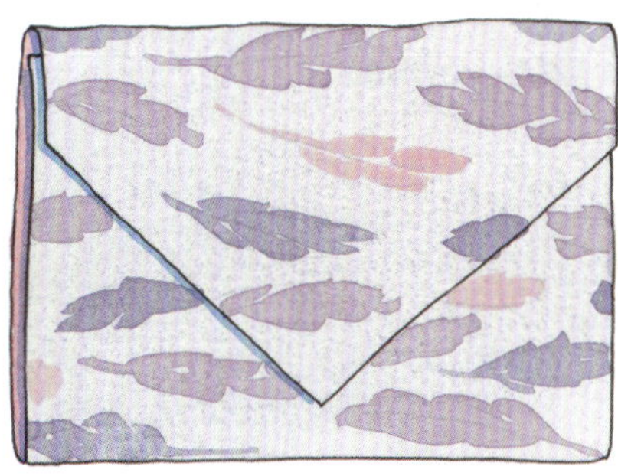

5 To mark where the magnetic clasp is going to go, fold the bag into its finished shape, fold the top flap over onto the outside of the main fabric and mark where the closing part of the fixing should go.

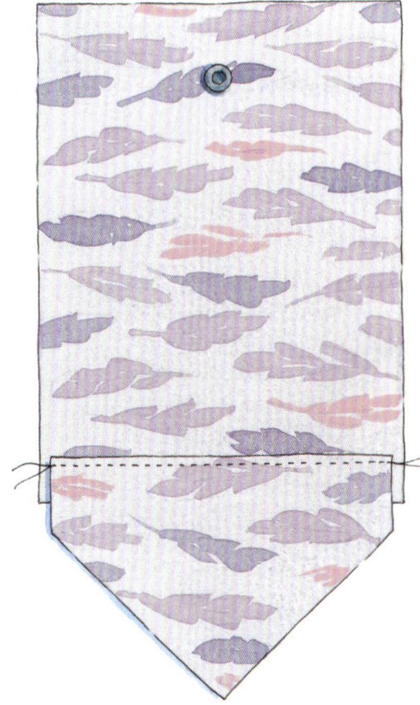

6 Open out the bag again and attach the second part of the fixing where you made a mark in step 5.

7 Sew ⅜in (1cm) side seams of the main and lining fabric pieces. Turn only the lining right side out and insert it into the bag pouch. Sew a ⅜in (1cm) top edge seam, leaving a small opening at the back to allow for turning.

8 Turn right side out, press the top edge, and topstitch to close the opening and finish off the bag.

ombré bedlinen

This is a great project for non-sewers. You start with plain white bedlinen and transform it using a dip-dyeing technique and stamps.

skill level: ●●

printing technique

dip-dyeing and eraser stamp (see page 10)

materials

Plain white cotton duvet cover and pillowcase

printing tools

Rubber gloves
Fabric dye for hand use in main color
Fabric paint in contrast color
Large bucket or plastic crate
Washing line or chair
Newspaper
Sponge
Pencil eraser

1 Wearing rubber gloves, prepare your fabric dye according to the manufacturer's instructions in a bucket or plastic crate large enough to fit your duvet cover without it being too creased.

2 As the dyeing technique involves starting with part of the cover in the dye and then gradually lifting it out to achieve an ombré, or graded, dye effect, you need a way of suspending the duvet cover in the dye. A washing line is ideal for this.

3 Wash and spin-dry your duvet cover and pillowcase and leave them damp before you start the dyeing process, then hang the duvet cover over your washing line or chair. Let's say that you want to leave ⅓ of the duvet cover undyed. Start by hanging it so approximately ⅔ of it is in the dye. Suspend the fabric there steadily for 20 minutes, then lift it out so just ⅓ is left soaking in the dye. Leave it there for a further 20 minutes. Finally, lift it out so only the last 6in (15cm) or so is left in the dye. Leave it for a further 20 minutes.

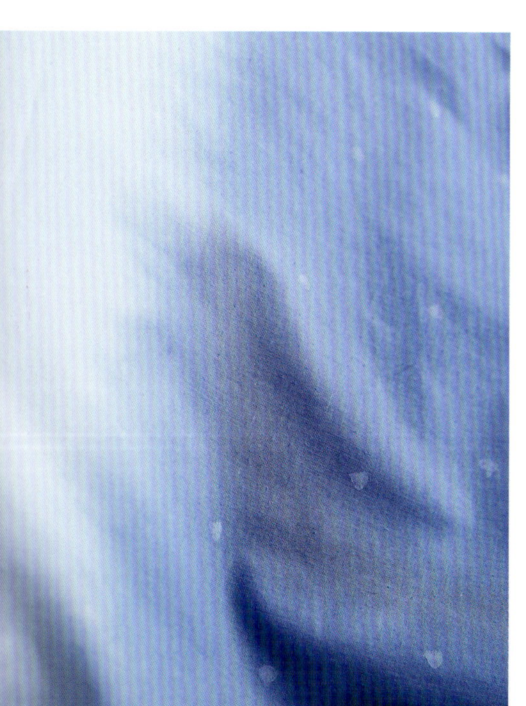

4 Remove your duvet cover from the dye and rinse out the excess dye under running water. You could use a hose in the garden or transfer the duvet cover carefully to a sink. Wring out, then dry gently to avoid dripping. Be very careful not to get any of the color on the undyed parts of the bedlinen. Once the water runs clear, wash the duvet cover in the washing machine. Make sure it is dry and ironed before you start to print.

5 To dye the pillowcase, dye the whole thing, leaving it in the dye solution for 40 minutes and stirring it around occasionally. Then rinse, wash, dry, and iron it.

6 To print the duvet cover, lay it out on a flat surface with some newspaper inside between the top and bottom layers so the paint doesn't come through.

7 Load a pencil eraser with fabric paint using a sponge, as described on page 10. Use this to build up clusters of dots, gradually applying fewer dots as you reach the undyed area of the duvet cover. For the pillowcase, line with newspaper and simply print dots all over.

8 Once you are happy with your design, iron the printed areas to set the paint and you are ready to enjoy your new bedlinen.

PRINTING TIPS

Dip-dyeing can be a bit messy, so be careful. You could do this outside so you can use a washing line to suspend the fabric in the dye. Embrace the imperfections that you will inevitably get—they make every piece unique.

cafetière cozy

This is a smart way to keep your coffee warm for hours. Thick industrial felt is available from felt specialists online and you can buy small sheets, which are perfect for a few craft projects like this one.

skill level: ●

printing technique
household item print
(see page 9)

materials

¼in (5mm) thick felt: 16 x 7in (40 x 18cm)

Leather strip or ribbon: ¼ x 20in (6mm x 50cm)

Paper

Scissors

Craft knife

printing tools

Wooden block: approx. 2½ x 1in (6 x 2.5cm)

Masking tape

Thin string or garden twine

Sponge

Fabric paint

1 Measure the height and circumference of the glass part of your cafetière and cut out a paper pattern that will wrap around the cafetière and overlap slightly. Cut out your felt so it is a little larger than the pattern. It's hard to print neatly over the edge of a piece of fabric: it's far simpler to print first, then cut to size afterward. Lay your felt on a flat surface ready for printing. These suggested measurements should fit most eight-cup cafetières.

2 To make your printing block, use masking tape to attach one end of a piece of thin string or garden twine to one wide face of your block, as described on page 9. Wrap the string tightly around the block till it is covered with a web of string, then attach the other end of the string to the face of the block where you started. You now have a printing block.

3 Use a sponge to coat the string lightly with fabric paint on the wide face of the block that is free of masking tape. Practice first on a scrap of fabric until you are confident you can achieve a clean, clear print.

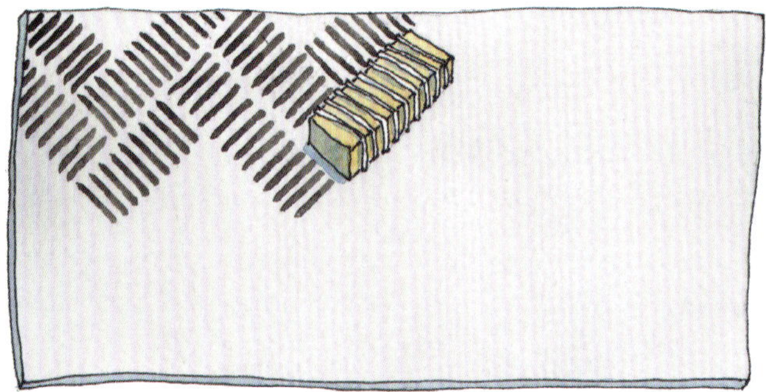

4 Make your first print in the center of the fabric on a diagonal and build up the herringbone pattern from there, turning the printing block through 90 degrees after each print.

5 Once you've covered the whole of the felt, iron it on a low heat to set the paint.

6 Now you can cut out the cozy shape using the paper pattern. To form the overlapping tab that will keep your cozy closed, use a craft knife or scissors to cut away two rectangles from one short side, leaving a tab in the middle that is approximately 1½in (4cm) deep by 3in (8cm) high.

7 Cut 2 vertical slits in the tab approximately ¾in (2cm) apart. Cut two matching slits along the other short side, approximately ½in (4cm) from the edge.

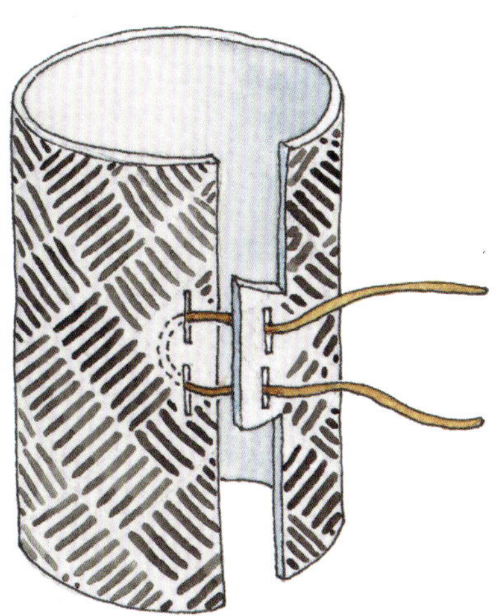

8 Thread your leather strip or ribbon from the wrong side of the felt through the slits on the side of the cozy without the tab. Wrap the cozy around the cafetière, thread the leather strip or ribbon through the slits in the tab and tie the cozy closed.

PRINTING TIPS

This print is made with a wooden block wrapped in string that's used to make a simple herringbone pattern. You can vary the angles of your lines, as well as how far apart they are spaced—experiment with the pattern to get a different result each time.

puffball purse

This bag has a lovely, soft outline and is a great size for your daily necessities. The print can be made using pre-cut foam shapes, easily available in your local craft store. Placing the shapes in a regular sequence creates a leaf pattern, and interest is added by making indents in the foam to make spotty sections.

skill level: ●

printing technique

foam stamps (see page 11)

materials

Leaf print motifs on page 117

Fabric template on page 121

Main fabric

Top cuff: cut two, 13 x 3in (33 x 8cm)

Bottom piece: cut two, 19 x 9in (48 x 23cm)

Handle strip: 20 x 1½in (51 x 4cm)

Lining fabric

Top cuff: cut two 13 x 3in (33 x 8cm)

Bottom piece: cut two, 19 x 9in (48 x 23cm)

Iron-on interfacing

Top cuff: cut two, 13 x 3in (33 x 8cm)

Matching thread

printing tools

Craft foam sheets or pre-cut foam shapes

Wooden or acrylic block, approx. 6in (15cm) square

Glue

Scissors

Fabric paint

1 Prepare your printing block as described on page 11, using pre-cut foam shapes or following the motifs on page 117 to cut out the foam shapes. Then, cut your main fabric to a slightly larger size than the pattern requires so that you can print a slightly larger area and cut it down to size later. Now print your fabric. Make sure that you space the rows evenly; you may need to practice on some scrap fabric first to get it right. Once the fabric paint is dry, iron the fabric to set the paint.

2 Cut out all of the pattern pieces in the main and lining fabrics, following the fabric template on page 121 for the bottom piece.

3 Following the manufacturer's instructions, iron the interfacing onto the main fabric top cuff pieces to stiffen them slightly.

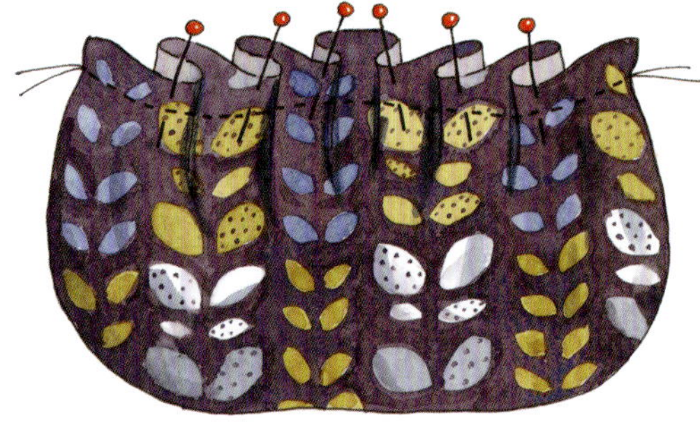

4 To make the pleats, on all of the bottom fabric pieces, find and mark the center of the fabric, then fold it in on either side of the center by ⅜in (1cm) and pin. Add two more folds on either side, they should be evenly placed and measure ⅜in (1cm) each; keep going until you have reduced your fabric top to measure 13in (33cm), matching the top cuff pattern piece.

5 Sew a line of stitching with a ¼in (6mm) seam allowance to hold the pleats in place. Repeat this process on all bottom pieces, main fabric and lining fabric.

6 With right sides together, sew the bottom pieces of the main fabric together (see page 110). Clip the corners (see page 112).

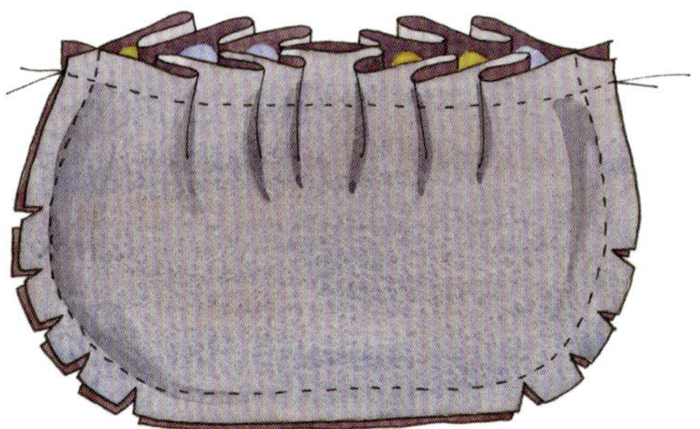

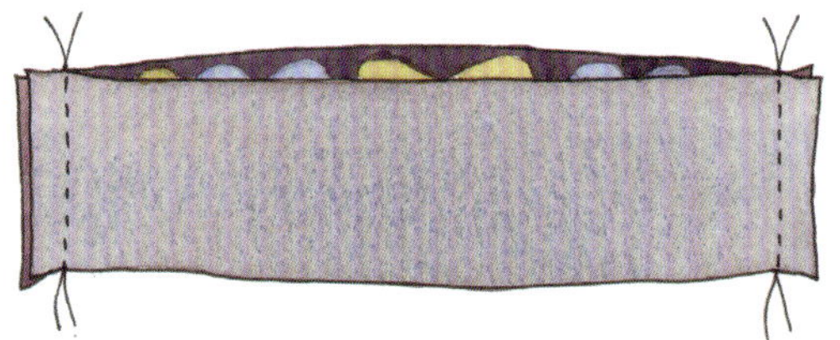

7 With the right sides together, sew ⅜in (1cm) side seams on the top cuff main fabric.

8 Turn the cuff right side out and place it inside the bottom pouch. Pin it to the top edge and sew in place with a ⅜in (1cm) seam allowance. Press the seams. Repeat this process with the lining bottom and cuff pieces.

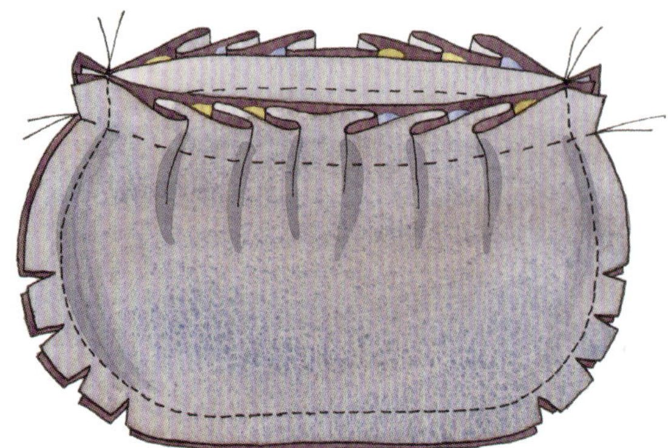

9 To make the handles, press ⅜in (1cm) seams on both sides of the handle fabric; then fold it in half to match up the edges and topstitch (see page 112) down both sides.

10 With the main fabric right sides together and the lining fabric right sides out, place the handle inside the main fabric and pin in place at the sides, insert the lining fabric and pin all around the top edge.

11 Sew a ⅜in (1cm) seam around the top edge (reverse stitch over the handle tabs for extra strength) and leave a small opening—4in (10cm)—in the back seam for turning right side out.

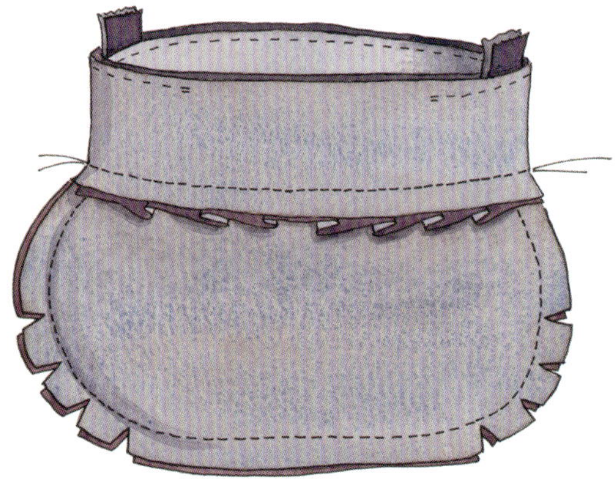

12 Turn the whole bag right side out, press the top seam, and topstitch a neat line of stitching to close the opening and finish the bag.

long satchel

This is a flat, body-hugging shoulder bag, big enough to fit all your essentials inside. A secure zippered main bag and easy-access front pockets make this a great bag to take out and about. The bag is printed with a fun daisy design.

skill level: ●●●

printing technique
eraser stamp (see page 10)

materials

Flower and stamen motifs on page 117

Main fabric

Bottom front: cut one, 11 x 13in (28 x 33cm)

Top front: cut one, 11 x 2½in (28 x 6cm)

Front pocket: cut one, 11 x 9in (28 x 23cm)

Back: cut one, 11 x 15in (28 x 38cm)

Lining fabric

Bottom front: cut one, 11 x 13in (28 x 33cm)

Front pocket: cut one, 11 x 9in (28 x 23cm)

Back: cut one, 11 x 15in (28 x 38cm)

Iron-on interfacing

Back: cut one, 11 x 15in (28 x 38cm)

Matching zipper, 12in (30cm)

Matching thread

Two eyelets—large enough to work with the trigger hooks

Two trigger hooks (dog leash clips)

Cotton tape, approx. 39in (1m)

printing tools

Rubber sheet or large eraser

Lino cutting tools

Fabric paint

Sponge roller

1 Cut out your main fabric slightly larger than the pattern pieces and press ready for printing. Prepare your eraser stamp as described on page 10 and print your fabric. Once the print has dried, iron the fabric at a high heat to set the fabric paint. Cut out your pattern pieces accurately and iron the interfacing onto the main fabric.

2 Take the front pocket pieces and, with right sides together (main and lining fabrics), sew a ⅜in (1cm) seam along the top edge (see page 110), turn right side out, press, and topstitch (see page 112). Place the made up pocket onto the right side of the main front fabric piece and sew with a dividing seam creating two front pockets.

3 Working with the fabric front piece that you have just attached the pocket to, place the zipper face down on the right side of the fabric and sew the zipper to the top edge, right sides together (see page 113). Now attach the inside lining to the zipper. Turn the main fabric over and sew the zipper to the top edge of the lining following the same line of stitches just made. Fold, press, and topstitch.

4 Sew the other side of the zipper to the small front top section of the main front piece of fabric. Lay the top fabric section facedown over the front of the zipper and sew along the zipper edge, fold the main fabric away from the zipper, and press. Lay the whole front section on the right side of the central lining and sew together with a line of stitches along the top edge of the zipper.

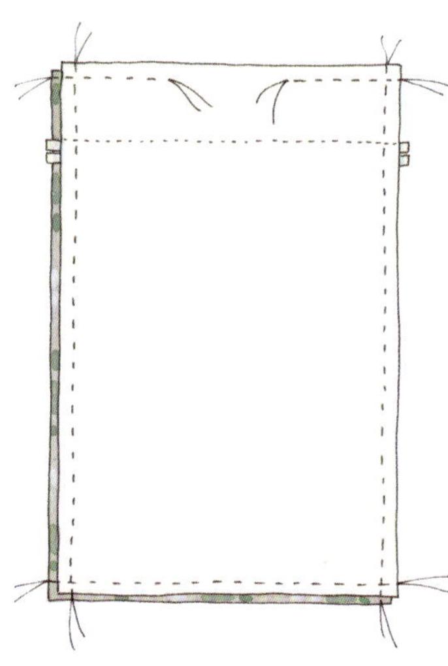

5 You can now attach the back panel to complete the bag. Place the constructed front section, right sides facing together, onto the main fabric back piece, pin, and sew a ⅜in (1cm) seam around the whole bag, leaving a small opening at the top for turning.

6 Trim the corners (see page 112) and turn the whole bag right side out. Flatten the bag, press, and topstitch a neat seam around the top part of the bag. Attach eyelets in each corner.

7 Cotton tape and trigger hooks are used to make the handles. Cut the strap to length, allowing an extra 4in (10cm) at each end to thread through the trigger hooks. Fold the strap back on itself at each end and sew in place with a square of stitches. Attach to the bag with the trigger hooks.

japanese fabric giftwrap

A super cute and environmentally friendly way to wrap your gifts, you can make your wrapping to any size you need, but a simple square of fabric can work wonders and can be reused again and again.

skill level: ●

printing technique

household item print (see page 9)

materials

Triangle print motifs on page 117
Fabric: 18 x 18in (46 x 46cm)
Pins, matching thread (optional)

printing tools

Wallpaper seam roller
Scraps of sticky-backed foam
Scissors or craft knife
Fabric paint
Sponge

1 This design is applied using a wallpaper seam roller with simple triangle shapes stuck all over it. Using the print motifs on page 117, cut out a number of small triangle shapes in several different sizes from the sticky-backed foam. Stick these onto the roller, as described on page 9, leaving small gaps between triangles.

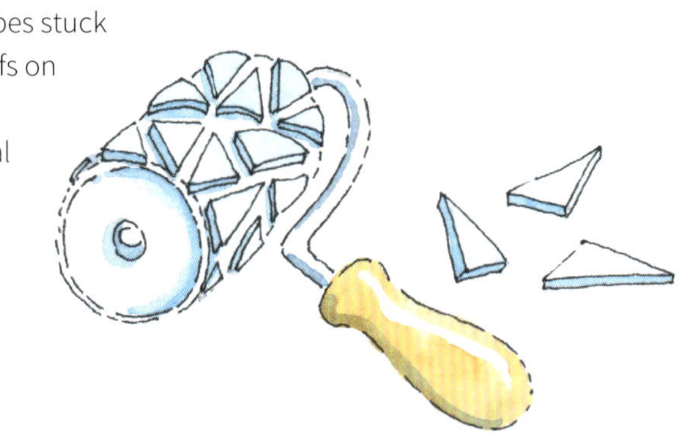

2 Iron your fabric, cut it to size and lay it on a flat surface ready for printing. You need to be able to run the roller across the whole piece in one go.

3 Load the roller with fabric paint using a sponge. Practice first on a scrap of fabric until you are confident you can achieve a clean, clear print.

4 Start at one corner of the fabric and carefully run the roller across. As the roller runs out of paint, you'll notice that you get a natural fade. Use this in your design either by making sure you always run the roller across in the same direction or by alternating directions. If you always go the same way, one side of your fabric will look more faded, but if you alternate, you get a more obvious striped effect. Reload your roller with paint each time you roller across.

5 When you are happy with your finished design, iron the fabric to set the paint.

6 Either leave the edges of your fabric as they are, so they fray naturally, or, with the wrong side facing you, fold under the raw edges along all four sides and pin (see page 111). Fold the fabric under a second time, so the raw edges are enclosed. Press the folds flat then sew a neat line of stitches close to the edge of the first fold to keep everything in place. Take care to stitch a neat right angle around the corners.

PRINTING TIPS

Using a roller with glued-on foam shapes is a great way to get a random pattern that can cover a large surface fast. You can vary your design by using different-colored paints and by making the most of the natural fade you get as you roll across the fabric.

backpack

This classic backpack is very practical and strong. Old belts were used to make the handles, and old key-chain clasps used for the front fixings. The two different fabrics used look great, but you can use one fabric all over if you prefer. Choose a strong fabric, so that you can really get some wear and tear out of this bag.

skill level: ●●●

printing technique
potato print (see page 9)

materials

Main fabric

Top front and back pieces: cut two, 12 x 10in (30 x 25cm)

Bottom front and back pieces: cut two, 12 x 4in (30 x 10cm)

Base piece: cut one, 12 x 6in (30 x 15cm)

Top side piece: cut two, 6 x 10in (15 x 25cm)

Bottom side piece: cut two, 6 x 4in (15 x 10cm)

Side pocket piece: cut two, 8 x 8in (20 x 20cm)

Flap piece: cut one, 12 x 12in (30 x 30cm)

Handle tab: cut one, 3 x 8in (8 x 20cm)

Lining fabric

Top front and back pieces: cut two, 12 x 10in (30 x 25cm)

Bottom front and back pieces: cut two, 12 x 4in (30 x 10cm)

Base piece: cut one, 12 x 6in (30 x 15cm)

Top side piece: cut two, 6 x 10in (15 x 25cm)

Bottom side piece: cut two, 6 x 4in (15 x 10cm)

Side pocket piece: cut two, 8 x 8in (20 x 20cm)

Flap piece: cut one, 12 x 12in (30 x 30cm)

Iron-on interfacing

Cut one, 12 x 6in (30 x 15cm)

Matching thread

2 x lengths of cord, 24in (61cm)

10 x large eyelets

printing tools

Potato

Sharp knife

Fabric paint

SEWING TIP

Before you start, make sure that your sewing machine can handle sewing through leather. Sew slowly and use a strong needle; try to find thin soft belts. You could also follow the same design with fabric belts.

1 There are many parts to this pattern, so it's best to cut them all out first, and then print on them. Once you have the pattern pieces, lay out the pieces that you are going to print on. Next, prepare a triangle design on your potato stamp as described on page 9 and apply the print. Allow the prints to fully dry before ironing all of the pieces on a high setting to set the fabric paint.

2 Iron the interfacing onto the base main fabric piece. Next, make up all the small elements of the bag. Sew the handle tab by pressing the edges inward by ⅜in (1cm) and top stitching (see page 112) both sides to give a neat finish. Make up the two strips for the front D-ring and key ring fitting. You can use either two strips of leather for this, or fabric tabs measuring 4in (10cm) long and as wide as your D-ring and key ring fittings.

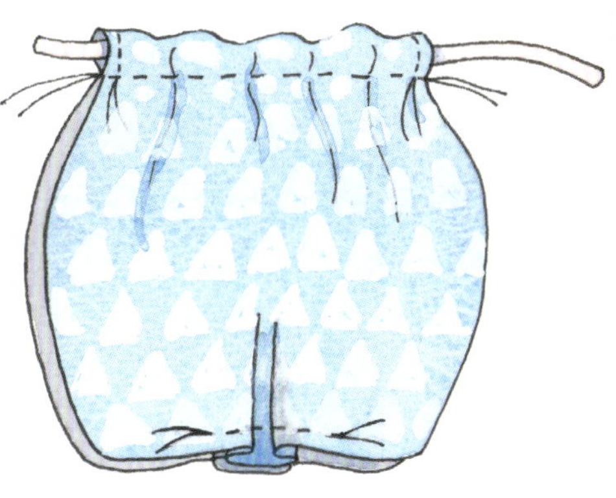

3 Working with the side pockets first, take the main and lining pieces and, with right sides together, sew the top with a ⅜in (1cm) seam (see page 110). Turn right side out and press—sew another line of stitches, ⅜in (1cm) down from the top edge, creating a channel to house elastic. Thread the elastic through the channel and attach it to one side with a line of stitches. Pull the elastic until the pocket top edge is 6in (15cm) long, pin, and secure to the other side of the pocket with stitches. To finish the pockets, make a central pleat at the bottom of the pocket, making the bottom edge measure 6in (15cm) to match the top edge, sew to secure. Follow this process for the other side pocket.

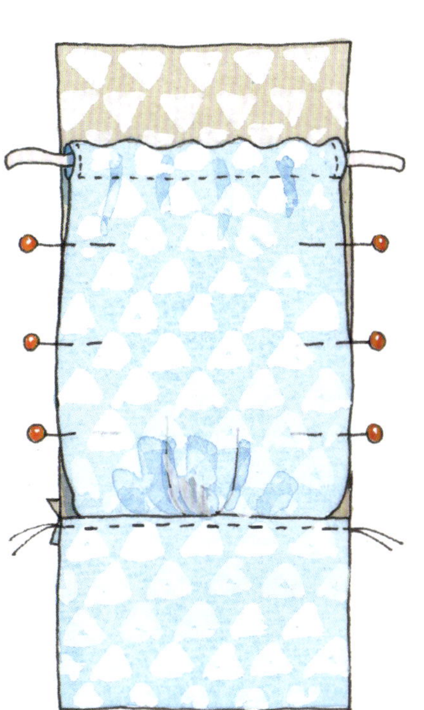

4 Take the top and bottom side panel pieces of the main fabric, place the made-up pocket piece on the right side of the top panel and pin in place to the bottom edge and all along the sides. Place the bottom panel on top of the pocket piece right sides together and sew closed with a ⅜in (1cm) seam, capturing the bottom of the pocket in the same line of stitches. Fold open, press, and topstitch (see page 112) the seam for strength. Do this for the other side panel.

5 Next, make up the back piece of the backpack with the buckle ends of the belts. Cut off the buckle ends to 4in (10cm) long. With right sides together, sew the back panel pieces together with the buckles in place—lay the belt wrong side against the main fabric, right side facing upward—with a ⅜in (1cm) seam. Turn and press, and topstitch the seam to give extra security to the buckles.

6 The next step is very similar. Working with the front pieces, with right sides together and the D-ring loop in place in the center—facing toward the top edge of the bag—sew together the panels with a ⅜in (1cm) seam. Turn right side out, press, and topstitch.

7 You can now bring all of these elements together to make up the main bag. Sew the side seams first, with right sides together, and making sure to line up the join in the fabric and to capture the pocket edges within the side seams. Attach the base by sewing, with right sides together, the front bottom edge first and working around the sides and back—leave a ⅜in (1cm) gap at each end to allow you to attach the base to the side pieces.

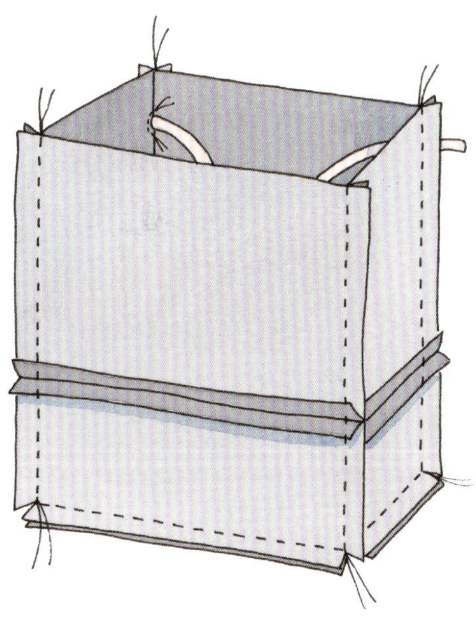

8 Make up all the lining pieces in the same way as you did for the main bag but without the pockets and buckles. Stitch together all the top and bottom parts of the bag, making up four complete panels, and press the seams. While you are sewing up the side seams of the lining, the cord for tying the top of the bag needs to be attached. On the back lining panel piece, 1½in (4cm) from the top, stitch one end of the cord in place facing it in toward the middle of the bag. Do this on both sides—one piece of cord per side. Now sew up the rear side seams, taking care to keep the cords in the center of the bag. Sew up the front side seams and attach the base with ⅜in (1cm) seams all round.

9 Take the main fabric and lining flap pieces and place them with right sides together, and with the key ring fitting at the center front edge pointing inward. Sew a ⅜in (1cm) seam all around the flap, leaving the straight top edge open. Clip the corners (see page 112) and turn right side out. Press and topstitch around the edges.

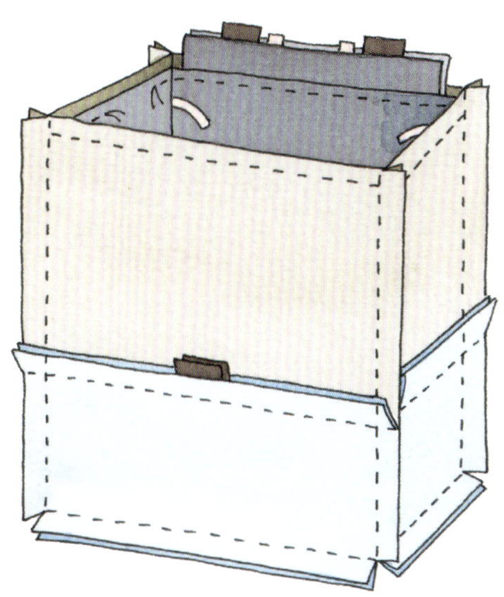

10 You now have all of the elements needed to make up the bag. The "pull-through" method is used to complete it. With the main bag pouch right side facing in, and the lining pouch right side facing out, insert the lining into the main bag. Pin the belt straps in place to the back main fabric, wrong side facing the fabric. Pin the handle tab in place in between the belts ends and pin the flap in place, right sides together, to the back panel of the main bag. Pin the lining all around the main bag top and sew around the top edge with a ⅜in (1cm) seam, leaving an opening on one side for turning. Take care when going over the back because it will be very thick with all the layers of fabric. Reverse stitch over the belts and handles a few times to secure them.

11 Turn the whole bag right side out through the opening and press the top seams, taking care to make sure the flap is held out of the way. Topstitch around the top edge to close the opening and give a neat finishing edge.

12 The final step is to make the eyelets for the cord to thread through to close the top. You will need five eyelets on each side. Mark the center front of the bag and place two eyelets an equal distance either side—work toward the back of the bag, placing the remaining four eyelets at regular intervals on each side. Follow the instructions from the eyelet manufacturer and practice on scraps first if you haven't used eyelets before. Thread the cord through the eyelets.

CHAPTER 2

stencils and screen-printing

tie-top curtains

These lovely curtains hang from easy ribbon ties with beautiful button embellishments. When you measure the width of your windows, add lots of extra fabric to make sure you get a soft, floaty effect.

1 Start by measuring your window. If you would like your curtains to be floaty and full, use double the window width. Whether you do this or not, add 1½in (4cm) to the width and 4in (10cm) to the top and bottom for your edges and hems. Cut out two pieces of fabric to the measurements you require.

skill level: ●

printing technique
screen-printing
(see page 13)

materials

Stem-and-leaves print motifs on page 118

Fabric: cut two pieces (see instructions)

Extra for ties or ribbon (see instructions)

Buttons (see instructions)

Pins, needle, matching thread, tape measure

printing tools

Letter-size (A4) screen

Sheet of letter (A4) paper

Craft knife

Parcel tape

Fabric paint

Squeegee

Hairdryer

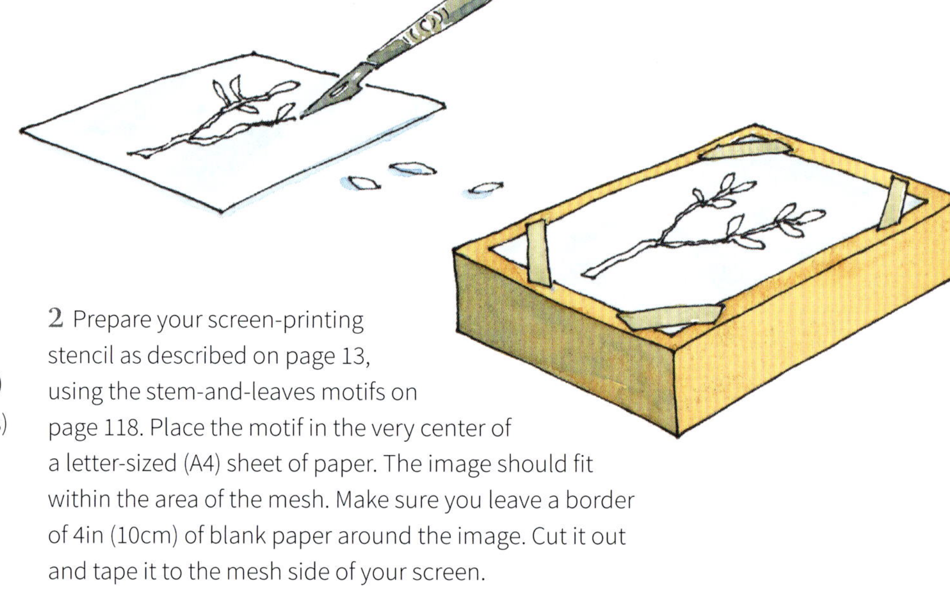

2 Prepare your screen-printing stencil as described on page 13, using the stem-and-leaves motifs on page 118. Place the motif in the very center of a letter-sized (A4) sheet of paper. The image should fit within the area of the mesh. Make sure you leave a border of 4in (10cm) of blank paper around the image. Cut it out and tape it to the mesh side of your screen.

3 Iron your fabric and lay it on a flat surface ready for printing. If your curtains are very long, you will have to print in sections, moving the fabric from time to time.

4 Lay your screen mesh-side down where you want the first print to go. Add a generous blob of fabric paint to the top of the screen, just above the design. Using the squeegee, scrape the paint across the surface of the screen in one steady action. Repeat a couple more times back and forth, then carefully lift up the screen. Dry your print with a hairdryer. Practice first on a scrap of fabric until you are confident you can achieve a clean, clear print.

5 Continue printing your fabric in this way to build up your design. Let each print dry before moving the screen to its next position. Once you have covered your fabric, leave the paint to dry fully, then iron the fabric to set the paint.

6 Next, decide how many pairs of evenly spaced ties you want at the top of your curtains. They need to be at least 10in (26cm) long and you need two ties at each point. You can use ribbons or make narrow fabric strips.

7 To make fabric strips, cut your fabric to 12 x 2½in (30 x 6cm), fold and press the sides and one short edge by ½in (1cm), then fold over lengthwise to join the long sides. Sew closed with a neat line of topstitches (see page 112) along both sides and the top (see page 113 for tips on making fabric ties).

8 To neaten the sides of the curtains, fold the edges over to the wrong side by ½in (1cm), press, then fold the edges again by ½in (1cm). Press again, then stitch neatly along the first fold.

9 Neaten the tops of the curtains by folding them first by ½in (1cm), then by 2in (5cm). Pin in place.

10 Now you can attach your ties to the tops of the curtains. Tuck them in pairs, facing downward and evenly spaced, under the pinned hem. Stitch neatly along the first fold, securing all the ties and closing the hem.

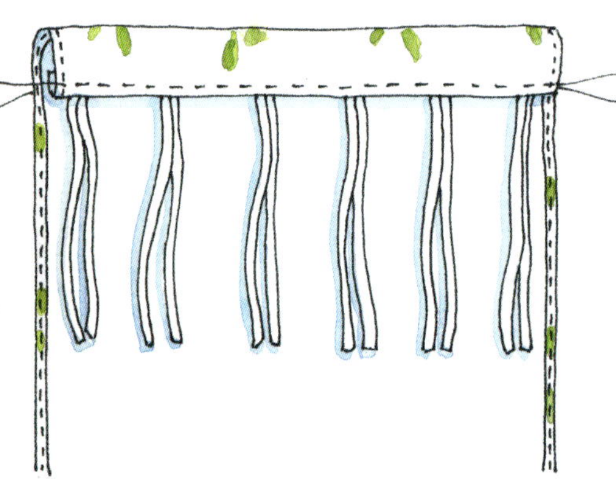

11 Fold the ties upward and sew another line of stitches along the top edge. This secures the ties in their final position and adds extra strength.

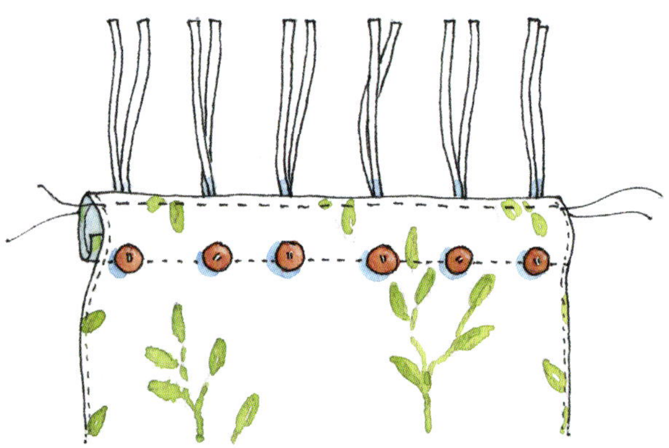

12 Hand-sew a button to the front of the curtains at the bottom of each pair of ties, for decoration.

13 To hem the bottom of the curtains, hang them in position at the window and pin up the bottom of each so they match. Take the curtains down and fold the edge over to the wrong side, first by ½in (1cm), then by 2in (5cm). Press, then sew in place to finish.

full-length apron

Every maker needs a stylish apron to protect their clothes and simply to look wonderful! Whether for your kitchen or your craft room, this easy-to-make fully-lined apron is perfect for your needs.

skill level: ●●●

printing technique
screen-printing (see page 13)

materials

Large leaf print motif on page 119
Fabric templates on page 123

Main fabric
Apron: cut one, 36 x 28in (90 x 70cm)
Pocket: cut one, 20 x 12in (50 x 30cm)

Lining fabric
Apron: cut one, 36 x 28in (90 x 70cm)
Pocket: cut one, 20 x 12in (50 x 30cm)

Cotton tape: approx. 2 x 79in (5cm x 2m)
Tailor's chalk
Scissors, pins, needle, matching thread, tape measure

printing tools

Letter-sized (A4) screen
Plain paper
Craft knife
Parcel tape
Fabric paint
Squeegee

1 Prepare your screen-printing stencil as described on page 13, using the leaf motif on page 119. Place the motif in the very center of your sheet of paper. The image should fit within the area of the mesh, make sure you leave a border of 4in (10cm) of blank paper around the image.

2 Turn your screen mesh-side up and place your paper stencil on top. Make sure the motif is in the center, then use parcel tape around the edges to attach it.

3 Iron your fabrics and cut them to size, then cut them out using the templates on page 123.

4 Once your screen and stencil are ready, practice on a scrap of fabric until you are confident you can achieve a clean, clear print. Lay your screen stencil side down on the apron fabric, put a generous blob of paint on the screen above the image, then drag the paint across the surface with even pressure using a squeegee. Drag the paint back and forth across the image two or three times. Your first pass of ink will secure the paper stencil in place to the mesh side of the screen. Carefully lift up the screen and reposition it for the next print.

PRINTING TIPS

This is a great way to try out screen-printing and work with a large repeatable pattern. If you don't want to screen-print, you could just use this as a simple stencil and use a sponge to apply the paint.

5 Build up your design by printing the leaf motif randomly. Leave plenty of space between each leaf and rotate each one to add variety and interest. Remember to print a leaf on the pocket piece, too. Once the paint is dry, iron the fabric to set the paint.

6 To make up the apron, start with the pocket. With the main and lining fabric pieces right sides together, leave a ½in (1cm) seam allowance (see page 110) and sew all around the edges. Leave a small opening in the bottom edge for turning.

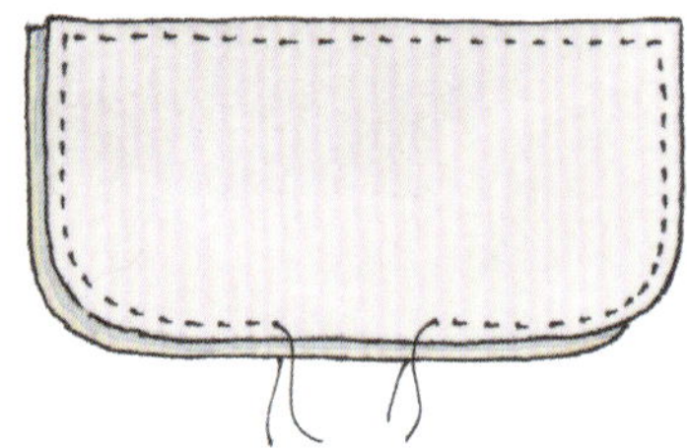

7 Trim the corners of the pocket and turn to the right side through the opening. Hand-sew the opening closed.

8 To attach the pocket to the front of the apron, use the template on page 123 and mark in chalk where the pocket should go. Pin the pocket in place, then sew a neat line of stitches around the sides and bottom edge to secure the pocket. Reverse-stitch a few times at the top corners of the pocket as this is where there will be the most stress. Sew a line of stitches down the center and through the apron to divide the pocket into two sections.

9 Now pin the neck strap and the ties made from the cotton tape in place. Cut the neck strap longer than you need, then you can adjust it with a knot once it is finished. Pin the ends of the neck strap to the top of the apron about 2in (5cm) from the corners, with the loop of the strap facing down. Cut the ties so they are long enough to go around you and tie at the back. Pin the ties to the sides of the apron about 2in (5cm) down from the corners and facing inward.

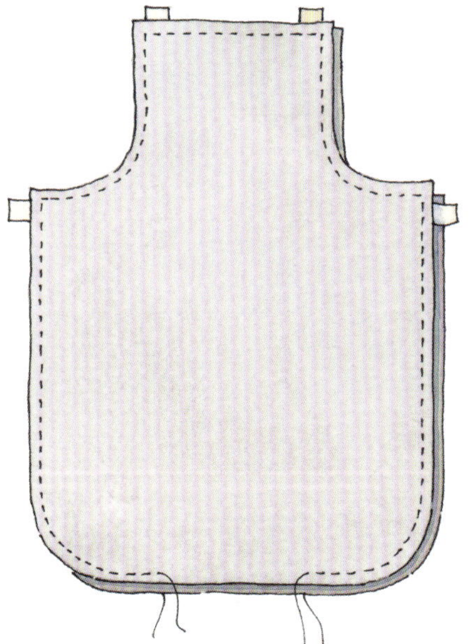

10 Place the lining on top of your main fabric, right sides together, and pin all around, making sure the strap and ties are tucked inside. Leaving a ½in (1cm) seam allowance, sew all around the edges. Leave a small opening in the bottom edge for turning.

11 Trim all the corners and clip the curves, taking care not to cut through the stitches (see page 112). Turn the apron to the right side through the opening. Push out all the corners and press the edges flat. Topstitch (see page 112) a neat line of stitches all the way around the apron, closing the opening at the bottom edge as you go.

giant floor pillows

These square pillows are great for providing extra comfy seating. You can stack them high and always have a spare for an unexpected guest.

skill level: ●●

printing technique

stencil (see page 12)

materials

Large pillow

Geometric print motif on page 118

Fabric: 54 x 28½in (142 x 72cm)

Zipper: 30in (76cm)

Foam pillow form: 20 x 20 x 6in (50 x 50 x 15cm) or polyester fiberfill

Small pillow

Fabric: 40 x 20.5in (102 x 52cm)

Zipper: 22in (55cm)

Foam pillow form: 15 x 15 x 6in (38 x 38 x15cm) or polyester fiberfill

Tailor's chalk

Scissors, pins, zipper foot, matching thread

printing tools

Freezer paper or plain paper

Craft knife

Temporary spray adhesive (optional)

Sponge roller

Fabric paint

Hairdryer

1 Prepare your stencil as described on page 12, using the motif on page 118. Print out the motif and trace it onto freezer paper or plain paper. Repeat the motif across the whole piece of paper, then use a craft knife to cut out the shapes.

2 Iron your fabric, cut it to size and lay it on a flat surface ready for printing.

3 Place the stencil in one corner of the fabric. If your stencil is made from freezer paper, you can iron it in place, otherwise lightly spray the back with temporary spray adhesive.

4 Use the roller to sponge the fabric paint onto the fabric through the stencil. Practice first on a scrap of fabric until you are confident you can achieve a clean, clear print.

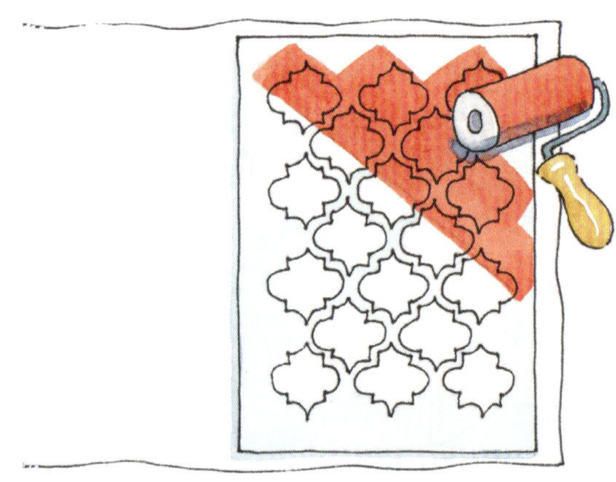

5 Use a hairdryer to dry the paint, then peel the stencil away from the fabric and reposition it, lining it up to the already-printed area to continue the design seamlessly. When you are happy with your finished design and all the fabric has been printed, iron the fabric to set the paint.

6 To make the pillow cover, you first need to attach the zipper to the short edge of the fabric (see page 113). Lay your closed zipper face down on the right side of the fabric along one short edge. Using your zipper foot, sew the right edge of the zipper in place with a line of stitches close to the teeth.

7 Fold over the other short edge of the fabric and line up the edge with the other side of the zipper. Sew this side of the zipper as you did in step 6.

8 Turn the fabric to the right side and press the zipper seams flat to get a nice finish.

9 Turn the pillow cover inside out again to complete the rest of the pillow. Leaving a ½in (1cm) seam allowance (see page 110), sew the long edges (the side seams) closed.

10 Next you need to give your pillow cover its boxy shape. Working on the wrong side, fold the fabric so that the seam with the zipper is flattened, the zipper is in the center, and two protruding corner triangles are created. For both sizes of pillow, measure 3in (7.5cm) from the point of each triangle and mark with tailor's chalk. From this point measure and mark two vertical lines 6in (15cm) long. These will be your stitch lines. Pin the corners in place. Repeat for the other two corners, then sew along your four stitch lines.

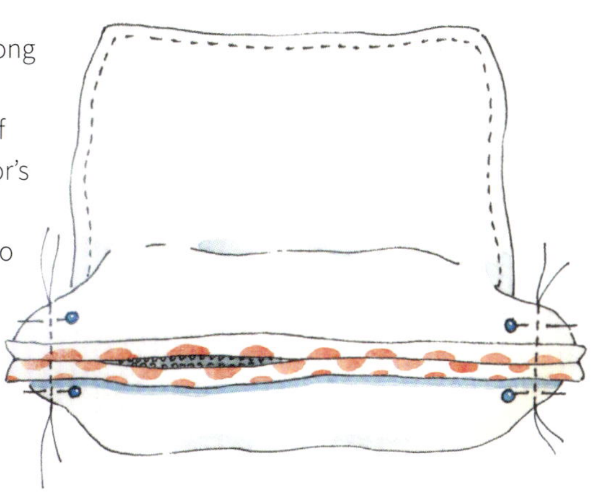

11 Turn your pillow cover to the right side and insert a foam pillow form through the open zipper or stuff with polyester fiberfill.

nest of tables

Upcycling old furniture is a great way to give new life to a piece of furniture you have fallen out of love with. This idea capitalizes on the natural color and grain of the wood. These show through, making them part of the design, but you could also follow the same technique using a painted item.

skill level: ●●

printing technique

masking tape stencil (see page 13)

materials

Nest of tables

Clear varnish or stain (optional)

printing tools

Tape measure

Set square

Chalk

Craft knife

Masking tape

Newspaper

Scissors

Spray paint in a contrasting color to your tables

Clear spray varnish

1 This design is applied using the masking tape stencil technique described on page 13. Make sure the furniture you are going to stencil has a clean, dry surface. If it needs to be revarnished or stained, do this at least 24 hours in advance.

2 This design was laid out by eye, not by measuring perfectly. Use a set square only as a rough guide; don't spend too much time worrying about precise measurements. Divide the surface of your piece with equally spaced vertical lines marked in chalk. It doesn't matter how far apart they are, as long as they are equally spaced. Now mark dotted lines parallel to and centrally between the first lines.

3 Cut the end of a piece of masking tape perfectly square and attach it so its bottom left corner is lined up with one of the dotted lines. Cut the other end of the tape so it is perfectly square and its top edge is lined up with the nearest vertical line. Now stick a second piece of masking tape over the left-hand end of the first piece and at a 90-degree angle to it. The second piece of masking tape will meet the vertical line to its left at a 45-degree angle. This gives you your first "V".

PRINTING TIPS

This is a clever and simple way of setting out a design, using the width of the masking tape as the basis of your pattern.

4 Continue adding lengths of masking tape in the same way until the surface of the piece is covered with zigzags. Worry less about accuracy and more about the overall design looking straight. The spacing between the zigzags is up to you—just try to make it the same all over. Continue your masking tape over the edges of the piece of furniture and make sure it is stuck down securely so you get nice crisp edges to your painted design.

5 Use newspaper attached with masking tape to cover any parts of the furniture you don't want to get paint on—in this case, the table legs.

6 Prepare an area for spray-painting. It's best to spray-paint outside or in a very well-ventilated area. This design uses gold spray paint to complement the dark wood of the tables, but if you have a light-colored wood, a darker color of spray paint would work better. Spray your prepared furniture with two or three light coats of spray paint or until you are happy with the color and coverage you have achieved. Leave to dry completely, following the paint manufacturer's instructions.

7 Slowly peel away all the tape, taking great care not to peel away the paint or damage the original surface. If you need to touch up any areas, do so by spraying a small amount of the paint into a disposable pot, then use a paintbrush to touch up the areas that need it. If required, you can lightly scrape away any small bleeds of paint with a craft knife. Once you are happy with the design, again working outside or in a well-ventilated area, spray a few coats of clear varnish over the surface of the furniture—and you have finished.

roll storage

This is a neat little idea for storing loose picnic cutlery, but you could apply the same idea to storage bags for knitting needles, paintbrushes, or craft tools. You can adjust the size for whatever you require.

skill level: ●●●

printing technique
stencil (see page 12)

materials

Cutlery motifs on page 118

Main fabric

Cut one, 16½ x 10½in (42 x 27cm)

Lining fabric

Main panel: cut one, 16½ x 10½in (42 x 27cm)

Pocket piece: cut one, 16½ x 6in (42 x 15cm)

Cotton tape for handles, approx. 30in (76cm)

Matching thread

printing tools

Freezer paper or parchment paper and low-tack spray

Fabric paint

Sponges

Sharp knife

1 Prepare your stencil as described on page 12. Prepare your fabric by cutting it to size and ironing it. Apply your print design, and once the paint has dried fully, iron the fabric on a high heat to set the paint.

2 Fold your pocket piece in half, press, and topstitch (see page 112) the top edge. Place the pocket piece on top of the main lining piece, pin it to hold it in place, and sew dividing lines where you need them for your specific requirements.

3 Cut the cotton tape into three pieces: two 12in (30cm), and one 6in (15cm) long for the handle. On the main fabric, attach the tie strip facing toward the right-hand side of the fabric, 10in (26cm) in from the right edge and 5in (13cm) up from the bottom edge. Sew it in place with a square of stitches. Pin the handle and the other tie strip in place to the left-hand side of the main fabric. Pin the tie in the center and evenly place the handle's ends to either side.

4 With right sides together, sew the main fabric to the lining fabric with a ⅜in (1cm) seam, making sure to catch the handle and the dividing pocket piece in all of the seams. Leave a 4in (10cm) gap in the stitching at the end of the fabric without the handles.

5 Trim the corners (see page 112), turn right side out, and poke out the corners so that they're correctly shaped. Flatten and press the bag. Topstitch around the edges to close the opening and finish with a neat edge.

simple round pillow

This lovely vintage-inspired pillow shape is so easy to make and adds a bit of timeless class to any chair. It consists of nothing more than two circles of fabric and a couple of buttons. You can, of course, adapt the size to suit your needs.

skill level: ●

printing technique

stencil (see page 12)

materials

- Flower print motifs on page 120
- Fabric: cut two, 20 x 20in (50 x 50cm), plus a scrap for covering button
- 2 buttons, at least 1in (25mm) diameter
- Pillow filling or filling recycled from an old pillow
- Sheet of paper
- Pair of compasses (optional)
- Scissors
- Needle, pins, matching thread

printing tools

- Freezer paper or plain paper
- Craft knife
- Temporary spray adhesive (optional)
- Fabric paint in two colors
- Sponge
- Hairdryer

1 Iron your fabric and cut out your fabric squares to size. You will cut them into circles once you've printed the top of the pillow.

2 Prepare your two-part stencil as described on page 12, using the flower motifs on page 120.

3 You are only going to print one of the fabric squares. Lay it on a flat surface. You can start printing anywhere on the square. Position the first stencil on the fabric. If your stencil is made from freezer paper, you can iron it in place, otherwise lightly spray the back with temporary spray adhesive.

4 Sponge on the paint from the outer edge of the stencil in toward the middle so the center of the flower is as lightly colored as possible and the edges are bolder, using the photo on the right as a guide.

5 Use a hairdryer to dry the paint, then remove the stencil. Place the second stencil in place over your stenciled flower, keep it in place as before, then sponge on the darker paint, again sponging from the edge toward the center. Dry the paint and remove the stencil. Practice first on a scrap of fabric until you are confident you can achieve a clean, clear print with the two stencils.

6 Place your next flower so it slightly overlaps the first one. Position each stencil and sponge on the paint as before. Repeat until you have covered the fabric with printed flowers.

7 When you are happy with your design, iron the fabric to set the paint, then wash the fabric. Once it is dry, iron it again, ready to cut the pattern out.

8 Now you are ready to cut the fabric into circles with a diameter of 16in (40cm). Either use a pair of compasses set to 8in (20cm) to draw a circle on a piece of paper, or draw around an object that is 16in (40cm) diameter. Place your paper circle on top of each fabric square, pin it in place, and cut around it.

9 Place the two fabric circles together, right side to right side and pin. Leaving a ½in (1cm) seam allowance (see page 110), sew around the edge. Leave a small opening for turning and filling. Clip at intervals along the seam (see page 112), taking care not to cut through the stitches.

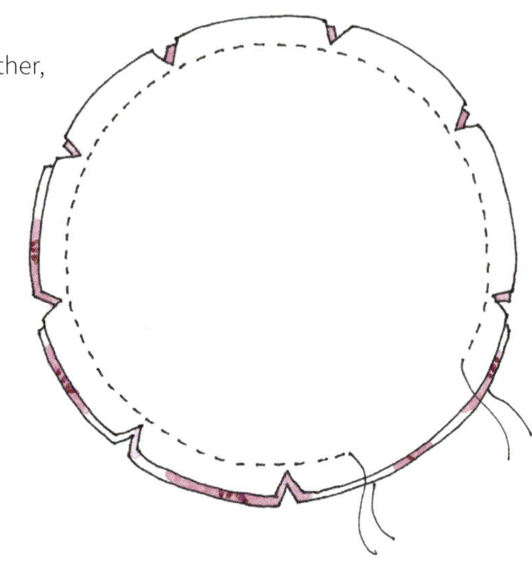

10 Turn to the right side through the opening, then stuff your pillow to the desired firmness with pillow filling. Hand-sew the opening closed, then plump up the pillow so the filling is even.

11 You can use any buttons for the center but this design uses a fabric-covered button for the front and a plain button for the back. See page 114 to find out how to cover a button.

PRINTING TIPS

This print is built up using two stencils and two colors. The first stencil gives the bottom layer of petals and the second stencil provides the darker details. The pattern on this design was made by randomly overlapping each flower, leaving unprinted fabric peeking through in just a few places. Washing the fabric after printing and heat-setting the paint stops the fabric from feeing heavy and stiff.

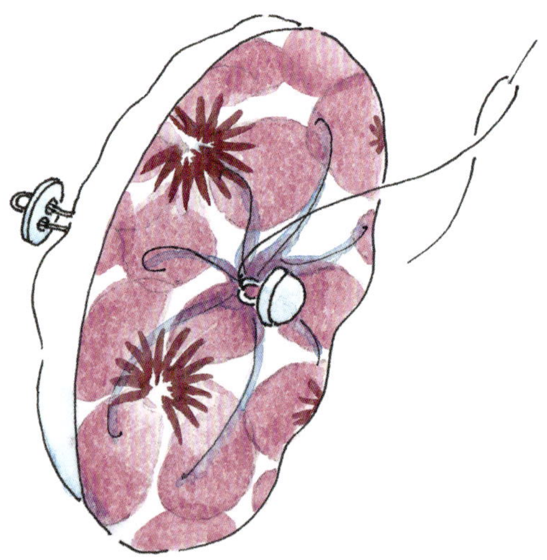

12 Find and mark the center of both sides of the pillow. Using a large needle, sew your covered button to the printed side at the center, then take the needle to the center back of the pillow and attach a second button there. Pull the thread tightly through both buttons and through all the layers of fabric, and lovely pleats will form.

fern-print coasters

This no-sew project is a simple introduction to screen-printing. Coasters are always useful for protecting your precious surfaces, especially if you make them from thick felt. They are a great housewarming gift and can be made to any shape or size. This project makes four coasters, cut into simple circles. It's easier to print the entire piece of felt, then cut the circles out afterward.

skill level: ●

printing technique

screen-printing (see page 13)

materials

Fern print motif on page 118
Thick felt: 12 x 12in (30 x 30cm)
Fine nylon mesh: 15 x 15in (38 x 38cm)
Paper
Pair of compasses
Scissors
Tailor's chalk

printing tools

Embroidery hoop: 10in (26cm)
Pencil
Screen drawing fluid
Paintbrush
Hairdryer
Screen filler
Old credit card or squeegee
Parcel tape
Fabric paint

1 If you are going to make your own screen-printing frame, follow the instructions on page 15. If you have a readymade screen, move straight to step 2.

2 You need to transfer the fern motif from page 118 onto your screen. Place the screen mesh-side down, on the photocopied and enlarged motif. Trace over the motif in pencil directly onto the mesh. Make sure to leave a 2in (5cm) gap all around the edge of the motif.

3 Now, with your screen mesh-side up, you can paint on the motif using the blue-colored screen drawing fluid and a paintbrush. The fluid has a runny PVA-type consistency. You need to achieve a good solid line—if it's too thin, your printing won't work. Remember, practice makes perfect. Leave the mesh to dry fully; you can use a hairdryer on a low heat if necessary.

4 Once your design is dry, you must coat your screen with screen filler. Do this with an old credit card or squeegee. Pour a blob of screen filler on the card and drag it across the screen, covering the surface with a thin, even coat of filler. Take care not to overdo this or the drawing fluid will start to dissolve. Just drag the card quickly and smoothly once or twice across the screen. You don't need to go right to the edges of the screen as these will be covered with parcel tape later on. Leave to dry completely, using a hairdryer on a low heat to speed things up.

PRINTING TIPS

This is a simple homemade screen-printing technique. You can make your own screen out of an embroidery hoop and nylon mesh (see page 15 for more details) or use a readymade screen. Practice lining up the repeat on scrap fabric before you print the felt.

5 Once the filler is completely dry, wash out the drawing fluid under running water. Allow the water to run over both sides of the screen and after a few seconds you should see the drawing fluid start to disappear. You may need to rub gently in some areas but be careful, as too much rubbing will ruin the screen.

6 Hold the screen up to the light to check the drawing fluid has completely vanished. The edges of your design should be clearly defined and clear, both of drawing fluid and of filler. Leave the screen to dry.

7 Now prepare your screen for printing by covering the edges with parcel tape so no ink can get through to the fabric in areas where it shouldn't.

8 To print your felt, lay it flat. Place your screen mesh-side down, on one corner of the felt. Put a generous blob of fabric paint on top and, using the credit card or squeegee, scrape the paint across the surface of the screen in one steady action. Repeat a couple more times, then carefully lift up the screen. If you've used too much paint or too much pressure, there will be bleeds of paint on your felt. If you haven't used enough paint or enough pressure, your print will be incomplete. Practice first on a scrap of fabric until you are confident you can achieve a clean, clear print.

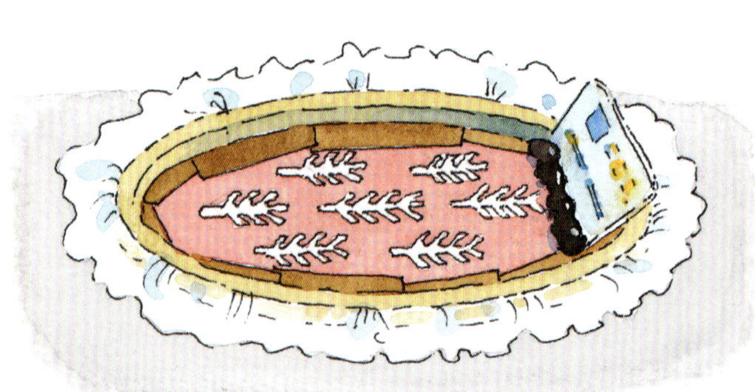

9 Work your way across the felt to build up the design.

10 As soon as you have covered the felt, wash your screen. Leave the paint to dry, then iron on a low heat to set it.

11 Make a paper template 4in (10cm) in diameter, using a pair of compasses, set to 2in (5cm). Cut out the template, lay it on the printed felt and draw around it with tailor's chalk. Cut the felt out carefully. Repeat until you've cut out all four of your coasters.

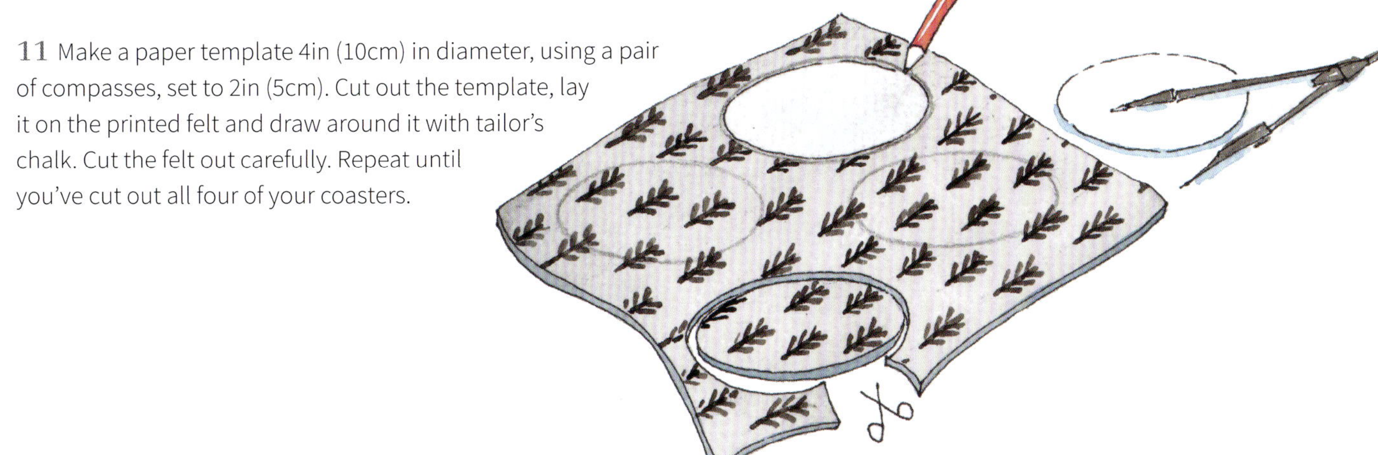

gathered purse

In this project, a simple piece of fabric is made to look far more interesting by using pleats. The handle style and pleating mean this bag has an elegant, flowing shape. A classic and simple damask-style repeated pattern is used for this bag.

1 Prepare your screen-printing stencil as described on page 13. Cut out the fabric pieces slightly larger than your pattern pieces to make the printing easier. Iron your fabric and then print. Once you are happy with your design, allow the fabric to dry completely before ironing to set the paint.

skill level: ●●●

printing technique
screen-printing (see page 13)

materials

Flower print motif on page 119
Fabric template on page 124

Main fabric
Cut two, 17 x 13in (43 x 33cm)

Lining fabric
Cut two, 17 x 13in (43 x 33cm)

Bias binding, approx. 5ft (1.5m)
Matching thread

printing tools

Freezer paper or waxed paper
Low-tack adhesive spray
Sharp knife
Sponge roller
Fabric paint

2 Cut out the fabric following the fabric template on page 124. To make the pleats on the lining fabric and main fabrics (four pieces), start by finding the center of the top edge and mark it. Fold in by approximately ⅜in (1cm) on each side of the center and pin. Moving along each side of the top edge, at even increments, fold and pin another four pleats until the whole top edge measures 8in (20cm). Topstitch (see page 112) a line of stitches to hold the pleats in place about ¼in (6mm) from the fabric edge.

3 With right sides together, sew a ⅜in (1cm) seam (see page 110) around the curved bottom of the main fabric pieces, leaving a 4in (10cm) opening at either end of the top of the fabric. Repeat this step with the lining pieces and clip the curves (see page 112) on both pouches.

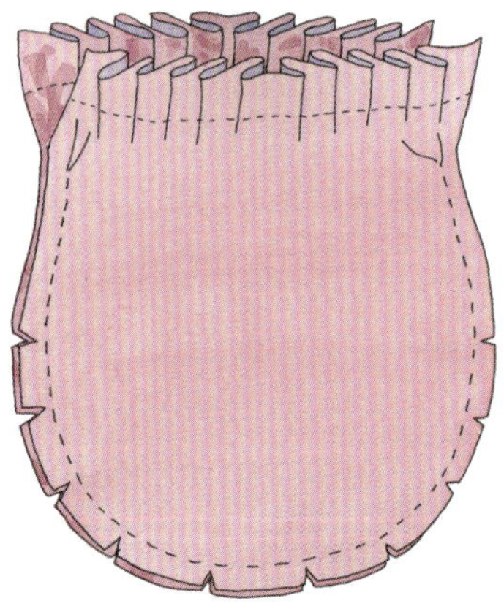

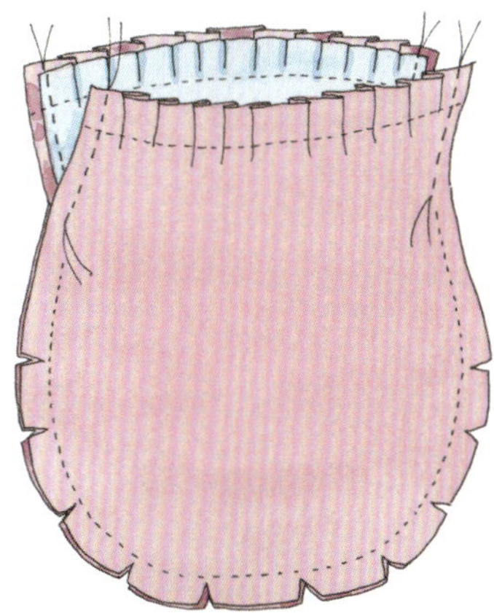

4 Leave the main fabric inside out, but turn the lining fabric right side in. Insert the lining into the main bag pouch, pin, then sew the side openings together with a ⅜in (1cm) seam—leave the gathered top edge open. Turn the bag right side out and press.

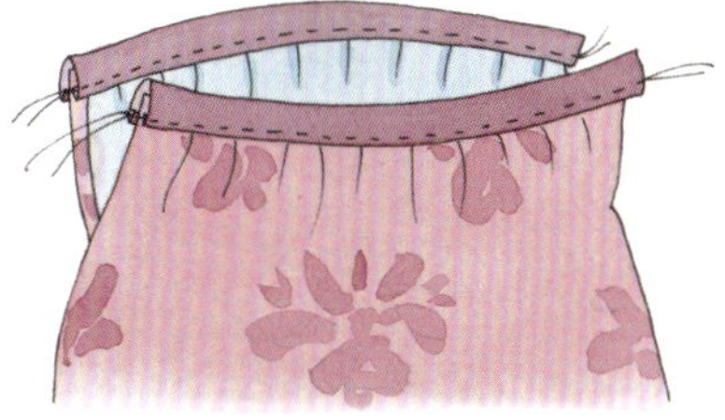

5 For the finishing touches, sew the matching bias binding over the gathered edges at the top of the bag—take care to sew through both sides of the binding (see page 113).

6 To make the handles, take one continuous line of bias binding and secure it in place at one side edge of the bag. Create a 16in (40cm) handle loop, which joins to the other side of the bag, continues straight down the bag edge, and back up the other side to meet the starting point of the bias binding. Make sure that you overlap the ends of the bias binding when it comes around to meet the starting point.

table runner

This runner is an elegant addition to any table. It's a great way to bring in design and color without having to print the whole surface of a tablecloth. Measure your own table and adjust the size of the runner according to your needs.

skill level: ●●

printing technique
screen-printing (see page 13)

materials

Leaf print motif on page 119
Fabric: 16 x 71in (40 x 180cm)
Scissors, matching thread

printing tools

Embroidery hoop: 10in (26cm) and fine nylon mesh fabric or readymade screen-printing frame
Pencil
Screen filler
Paintbrush
Parcel tape
Hairdryer (optional)
Fabric paint in 2 colors
Old credit card or squeegee

PRINTING TIPS

This is a simple screen-printing technique using painted-on filler to create your stencil. This project shows you how to make your own screen using familiar craft room objects. You can use the same technique with a readymade screen, too.

1 If you are going to make your own screen-printing frame from an embroidery hoop and nylon mesh, follow the instructions on page 15. If you have a readymade screen, move straight to step 2.

2 Prepare your design using the motif on page 119 and draw it directly onto the screen mesh in pencil, as described on page 13. Make sure to leave a 2in (5cm) gap all around the edge of the motif.

3 Using the screen filler, carefully paint all the areas around your design with an even coat. Once this is dry, it will act as a barrier, stopping any fabric paint seeping through onto the fabric in those areas. You don't need to paint right to the edges of the screen, just up to 2in (5cm) all around the design. The edges will be covered with parcel tape in step 4.

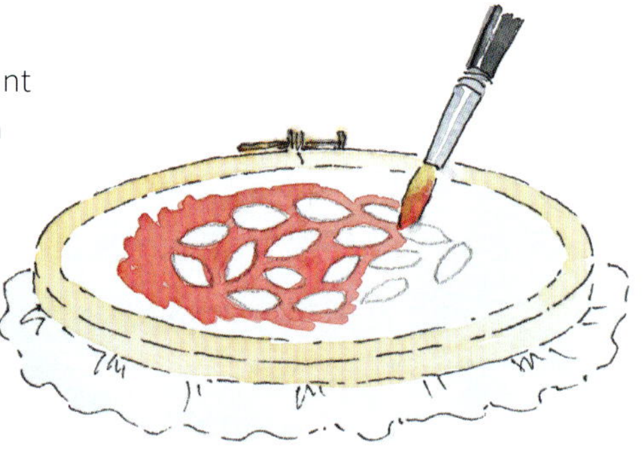

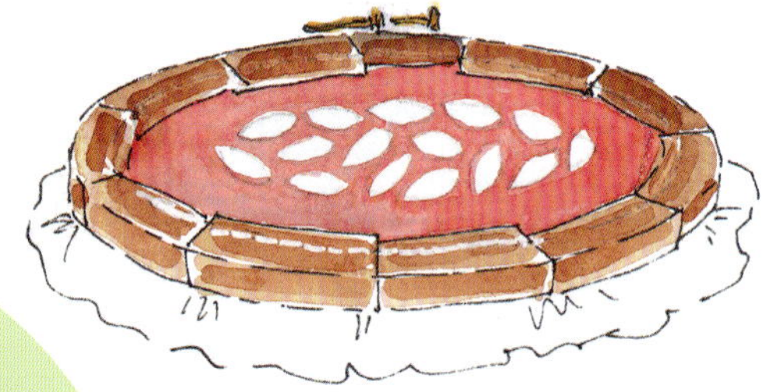

4 Leave to dry for at least an hour—you can use a hairdryer to speed things up. Once the filler is completely dry, cover the edges of the screen with parcel tape so no paint can get through to the fabric in areas where it shouldn't. Make sure the tape comes up around the edges.

5 Now iron your fabric and cut it to size: the measurements given include ¾in (2cm) all around for the hems—adjust your measurements if you need to. Lay the fabric on a flat surface ready for printing. If you can't lay it out in one long line, print half the fabric first, then turn it around to print the other half. Practice first on a scrap of fabric until you are confident you can achieve a clean, clear print.

6 The pattern is built up in rows, with the darker color printed first and the lighter color overlaid afterward. Lay your screen mesh-side down where you want the first print to go. Add a generous blob of the darker fabric paint to the top of the screen, just above the design. Using the credit card or squeegee, scrape the paint across the surface of the screen in one steady action. Repeat a couple more times back and forth, then carefully lift up the screen. Dry your print with a hairdryer.

7 Continue printing your fabric in this way to build up your design. Let each print dry before moving the screen to its next position.

8 Once you have covered your fabric with prints in this color, wash your screen thoroughly under running water and leave to dry. Repeat steps 6 and 7 using your light paint color and staggering the prints to achieve an attractive effect, using the photo as a guide. Make sure you wash your screen when you have finished and it will be usable for another project. When you are happy with your finished design, iron the fabric to set the paint.

9 Fold the raw edges of the runner to the wrong side by ½in (1cm), then fold them again by ½in (1cm). Press in place, then stitch neatly along the first fold. See page 111 for a clever way to finish the corners.

vine-leaf placemat

This placemat doesn't involve any sewing—just some clever cutting and an elegant wreath design.

skill level: ●

printing technique
stencil (see page 12)

materials

Vine wreath print motif on page 119
Fabric template on page 122
Felt: 16 x 14in (40 x 35cm), per placemat
Chalk pencil
Large and small scissors

printing tools

Craft knife
Freezer paper or plain paper
Temporary spray adhesive (optional)
Sponge
Fabric paint

1 Cut your felt to size and lay it on a flat surface. Cut the decorative edge along one short side before you do any printing. Using the fabric template on page 122 and a chalk pencil, draw the edging design onto the felt. Cut it out with a small pair of sharp scissors.

2 Prepare your stencil as described on page 12, using the wreath motif on page 119.

3 Place the stencil in the center of your piece of felt. If your stencil is made from freezer paper, you can iron it in place (use a low heat setting to avoid shrinking the felt), otherwise lightly spray the back with temporary spray adhesive.

4 Sponge the fabric paint onto the felt through the stencil. Practice first on a scrap of fabric until you are confident you can achieve a clean, clear print.

5 Once the paint is dry, peel the stencil away very carefully. Iron on a low heat to set the fabric paint.

PRINTING TIPS

This is a very delicate stencil, so take great care when cutting it out and ironing it on to the felt.

boxy weekender

This bag is all about folding fabric to create an interesting shape. Just one large rectangle of fabric is used to create a roomy box-shaped bag, which is great for an overnight visit, or just when you need a big bag! The print used on this bag is made with a large, layered stencil.

1 Prepare your stencils as described on page 12. Cut out your fabric pieces—choose a strong, firm fabric for your main piece because this will hold the shape better and you will not need to interface it. Use the sponge roller to print your fabric, allowing each layer to dry before printing the next. Once your design is dry, iron the fabric to set the fabric paint.

skill level: ●●●

printing technique

stencil (see page 12)

materials

Leaf motifs on page 120

Main fabric

Cut one, 40 x 22in (100 x 56cm)

Lining fabric

Cut one, 40 x 22in (100 x 56cm)

Iron-on interfacing: 40 x 22in (100 x 56cm) if necessary

Strong cotton tape for the handles, 99 x 1in (2.5m x 2.5cm)

Bias binding, 60in (1.5m)

Matching thread

Matching zipper, 22in (56cm)

printing tools

Freezer paper or contact paper

Sponge roller

Fabric paint

Scalpel or sharp knife

Dressmakers' chalk

2 Working on the main fabric, mark and pin the handles in place. Find and mark the center of the fabric, measure 5in (12cm) in from the short sides, and mark—this area will be the top of the bag and you do not want to sew handles to this part. Next, pin the handles in place to form a continuous oval approximately 6in (15cm) apart in the center of the bag, leaving the 5in (12cm) areas on either side clear.

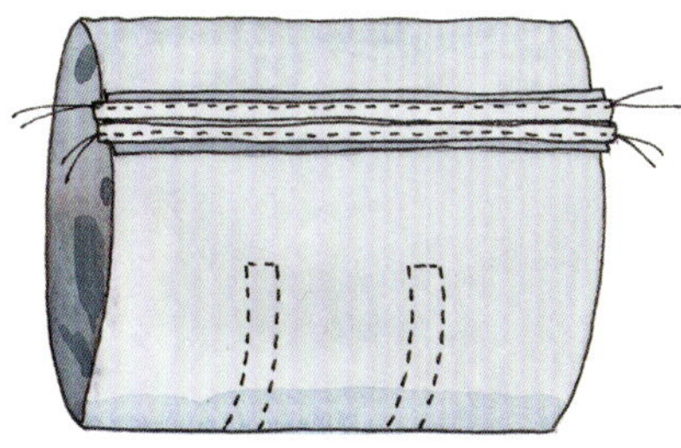

3 Sew the handles in place, remembering to reverse stitch over the ends because these will take the most strain. Now sew the zipper in place on the edges of the main fabric (see page 113).

4 Sew the lining fabric onto the zipper, making sure to follow the same line of stitching as for the main fabric, and enclosing the zipper between the main and lining fabrics.

5 Turn right sides out and press. Topstitch (over sew) a line of stitches along the line of the zipper for a neat edge. Take your time, because this edge will be very visible on the finished bag.

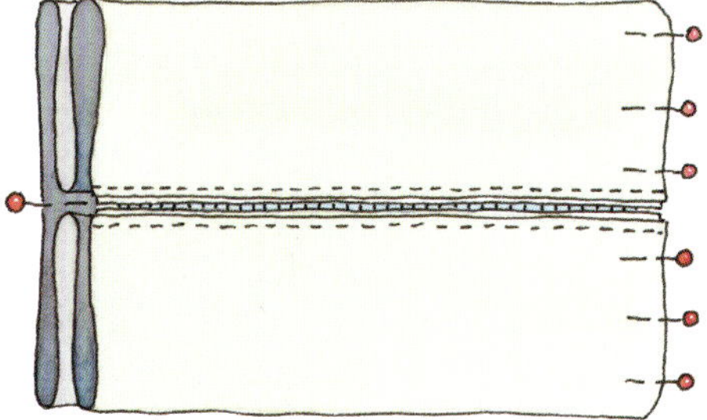

6 Turn inside out again so that the lining fabric is facing out and the main fabric inside. Fold all of the fabric flat with the zipper in the center—measure to make sure you are in the exact center. Mark the center on the bottom piece and mark the inside of the two edges with dressmakers' chalk or a pencil. Fold in the side edges to meet the center mark, creating four layers. Pin in place and repeat on the other side.

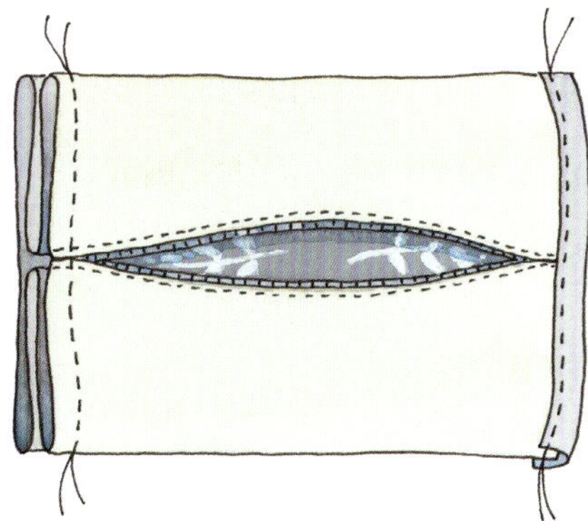

7 Sew through all the layers with a ½in (12mm) seam allowance to close (see page 110). Trim the raw edges and enclose by sewing bias binding (see page 113) or cotton tape over the edges. Turn the whole bag right side out and push out the corners to achieve the boxy shape.

square envelope pillow cover

This quick and easy stencil idea works brilliantly to spice up a pillow cover. I've made an envelope cover. It's easy as there are no zippers to fit! This project will make a pillow cover that will fit an 18in (46cm) pillow form but you can adapt the size if you want a bigger or a smaller one.

level: ●

printing technique
masking tape stencil (see page 13)

materials

Fabric:

Front piece: cut one, 19 x 19in (48 x 48cm)

Back pieces: cut two, 19 x 14in (48 x 35cm)

Pillow form: 18 x 18in (46 x 46cm)

Scissors, pins, matching thread

printing tools

Masking tape

Sponge

Fabric paint in three colors

Hairdryer

1 Iron your fabric, cut it to size and lay your front piece on a flat surface ready for printing. You are going to use masking tape to make the triangle shapes, as described on page 13, and you will print one triangle at a time. Practice first on a scrap of fabric until you are confident you can achieve a clean, clear print.

2 Mask along the edges of the largest triangle first and sponge on your paint, working from the point of the triangle downward. Sponge the paint on more heavily at the point and more lightly as you move down. Use a hairdryer to dry the paint, then remove the tape.

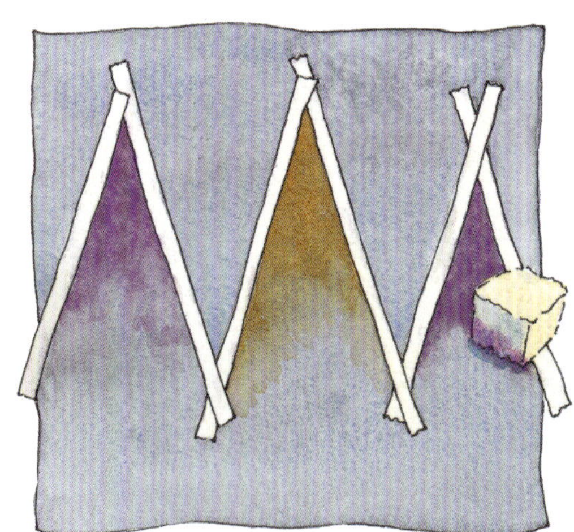

3 Mask off your next triangle so it overlaps the first, then sponge on another color paint in the same way. Repeat until you have a design you are happy with, then finish by ironing your fabric to set the paint.

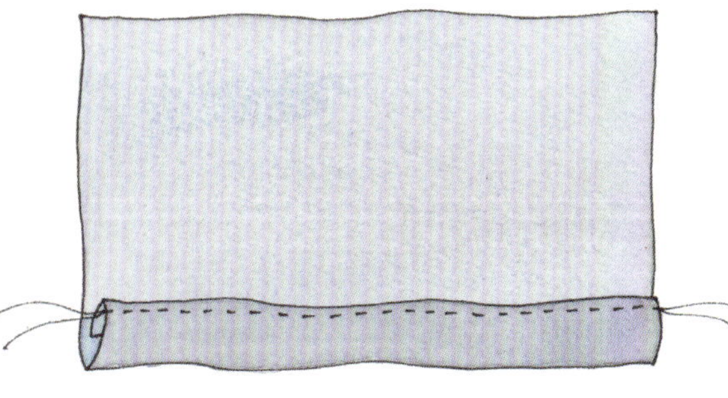

4 Cut out the two back pieces. With the wrong side of one back piece facing you, fold under the raw edge along one long side and pin. Fold the fabric under a second time, this time by 1½in (4cm), so the raw edge is enclosed. Press the folds flat, then sew a neat line of stitches along the first fold to keep everything in place (see page 111). Repeat for the second back piece.

PRINTING TIPS

This design uses masking tape to create the shapes. Paint is sponged on heavily at the top of the triangles and lightly at the bottom to give different tones. You could create many different looks this way, so get creative!

5 Now you are going to bring all three pieces together to make the pillow cover. Lay the front piece down right side up and place one back piece on top, right side down with its unfolded edge on the top edge of the front piece. Now lay the other back piece on top with its unfolded edge on the bottom edge of the front piece. The two back pieces should overlap in the middle. Pin all the pieces in place. Leaving a ½in (1cm) seam allowance (see page 110), sew along all four sides. Go carefully where the back pieces overlap as the layers will be very thick and harder to sew through. Trim away the four corners (see page 112), taking care not to cut through the stitching, then turn the pillow cover right side out and press.

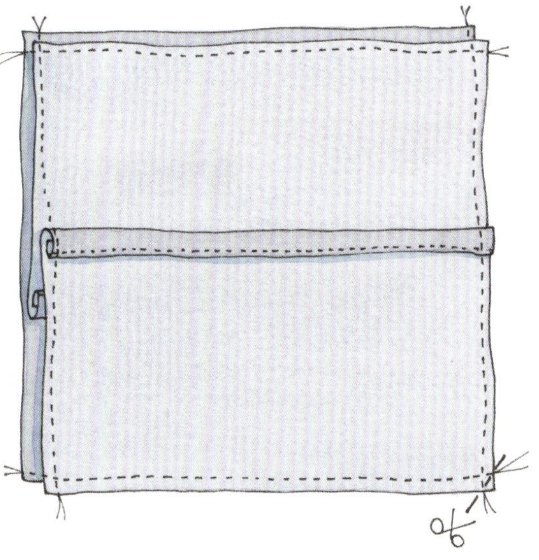

6 Insert your pillow form through the opening and you're done.

covered storage box

You can transform any box into stylish storage to complement your home decor. Why not make a set of different-sized boxes to hide all your clutter away?

skill level: ●●

printing technique
stencil (see page 12)

materials

Fabric (see instructions)
Box (either a shop-bought storage box, a shoe box, or another sturdy box)

printing tools

Paper doilies in various sizes (at least 6)
Stencil brush
Fabric paint
Paintbrush
Water-based glue

1 Remove any handles or other details, such as metal label holders. You will reattach those at the end.

2 Measure the length of each side of your box and add these measurements together. Add 8in (20cm) to the total—this is the fabric for the overlap—to give you the length of fabric you will need. Now measure the height of the sides, and again add 8in (20cm) to your measurements. This gives you the measurement for the depth of fabric you will need.

3 If your box has a lid, measure the top of the lid in exactly the same way. Add 4in (10cm) to these dimensions.

4 Iron your fabric, cut it to the sizes needed for the box and the lid, and lay it on a flat surface ready for printing.

5 You will need at least 6 doilies as they will get a bit clogged up with paint as you work. Start to stencil lightly through the doilies, as described on page 12, using the stencil brush to push the paint through the holes. This design uses simple overlapped semicircles, but you could choose other layouts such as the whole circle of the doily or just small sections closely overlapped. Experiment and practice first on a scrap of fabric until you are confident you can achieve a clean, clear print.

6 When you are happy with your finished design and all the fabric has been printed, iron the fabric to set the paint.

7 Start by attaching the fabric to one of the long sides of the box, leaving a bit of fabric for the overlap at the starting end. Now continue around the first short side, then the second long side, and finish at the second short side. Using the paintbrush, coat each side with glue as you get to it. Smooth the fabric in place, pulling it tight to avoid air bubbles.

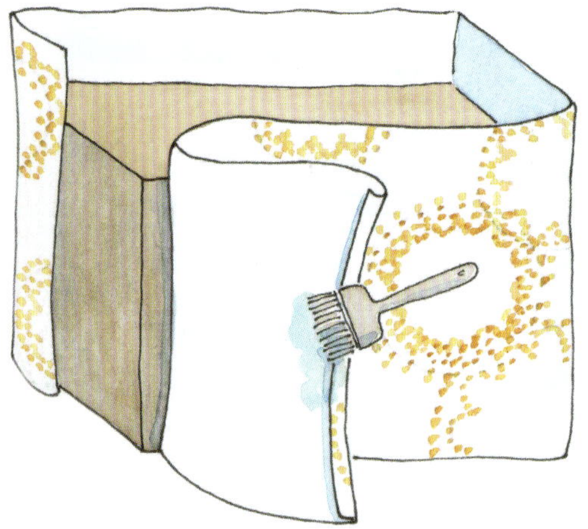

8 Fold over and glue a narrow hem along the end of the fabric to enclose the raw edge. Glue this folded edge neatly in place over the overlap at the starting end so you have a tidy corner.

9 Now you will fold the fabric over, gift-wrap style, so it also covers the bottom of the box. Apply glue to the bottom of the box then fold in the fabric along the two short sides and press it in place. Now fold in the fabric along the two long sides, making neat miters at the corners. Glue the fabric in place. When you fold in the fabric along the second long side, first fold over and glue a narrow hem, to enclose the raw edge. Allow to dry before moving on to the top edge.

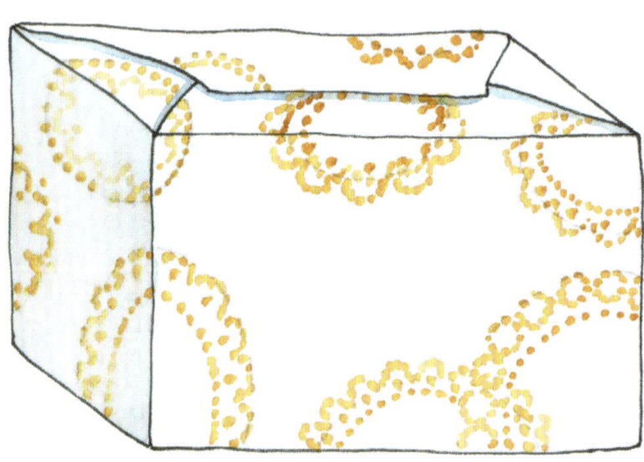

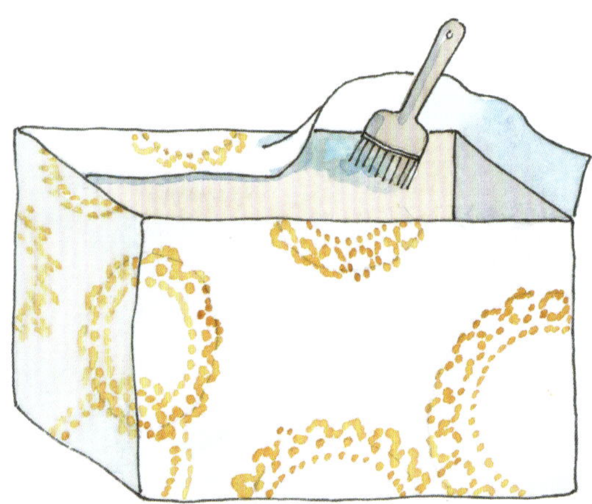

10 For the top edge of the box, trim the fabric if necessary so you have a neat 2in (5cm) overlap. Top up the glue along the top edge and continue it over the edge and onto the first 2in (5cm) of the inside of the box. Fold over the fabric to the inside, securing it in place.

11 Use this same process to cover the lid of your box, but this time start by gluing the top of the lid first. Take care on the inside corners to make sure the fabric isn't too bulky there or your lid won't fit back on.

12 Reattach any labels or label holders to your box, and you're done.

PRINTING TIPS

This is a simple idea that uses store-bought paper doilies as stencils; they are available from most supermarkets and from cake or party stores. Make sure you try out different patterns as some work better than others. Some doilies are too delicate and the stenciling doesn't come through very clearly—you need doilies with a nice, simple, cut pattern.

rounded shoulder bag

This is a very practical and cute little shoulder bag—it's perfect for throwing your essentials into and slinging over your shoulder when you're on the go. The print used on this is the ever-popular bird on a branch, a simple silhouette with added color spots for berries.

skill level: ●●●

printing technique
stencil (see page 12) and eraser stamp (see page 10)

materials

Bird motif on page 119

Fabric templates on page 125

Main fabric

Front and back: cut two, 11 x 9in (28 x 23cm)

Outer pocket: cut one, 11 x 7in (28 x 18cm)

Flap: cut one, 10 x 9in (25 x 23cm)

Lining fabric

Front and back: cut two, 11 x 9in (28 x 23cm)

Outer pocket: cut one, 11 x 7in (28 x 18cm)

Flap: cut one, 10 x 9in (25 x 23cm)

Iron-on interfacing

Front and back: cut two, 11 x 9in (28 x 23cm)

Outer pocket: cut one, 11 x 7in (28 x 18cm)

Flap: cut one, 10 x 9in (25 x 23cm)

Strap fabric (see step 6)

Matching thread

printing tools

Freezer paper

Sharp knife

Pencil with eraser

Fabric paint

Sponge

1 Cut out the main-fabric flap using the template on page 125. Prepare your stencils as described on page 12. Apply the stencils on the main-fabric flap piece. Print the berries using the eraser on a pencil as a stamp, as described on page 10. Once dry, iron on a high heat to set the paint.

2 Cut out the rest of your fabric and interfacing pieces using the templates on page 125. Iron the interfacing onto the main fabric pattern pieces. Sew the darts closed on all of the main and lining fabric pieces—to do so, fold the fabric right sides together, line up edges and sew a ⅜in (1cm) seam to close the darts.

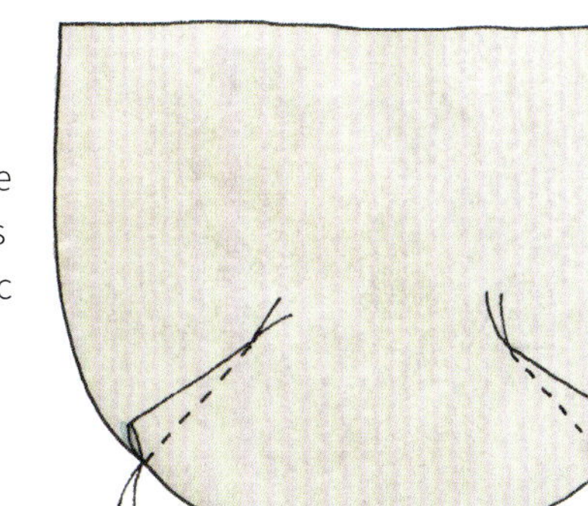

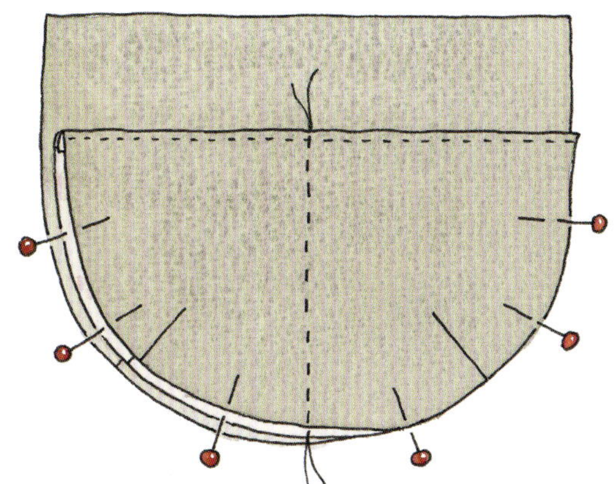

3 With right sides together, sew the outer pocket pieces (main fabric and lining) together along the top edge with a ⅜in (1cm) seam (see page 110). Turn right side out, press the seam, and topstitch (see page 112) along the top edge for a neat finish. Pin the made up pocket piece to the main front fabric piece, making sure to line up the darts, and then sew it in place with a central seam, creating two pockets.

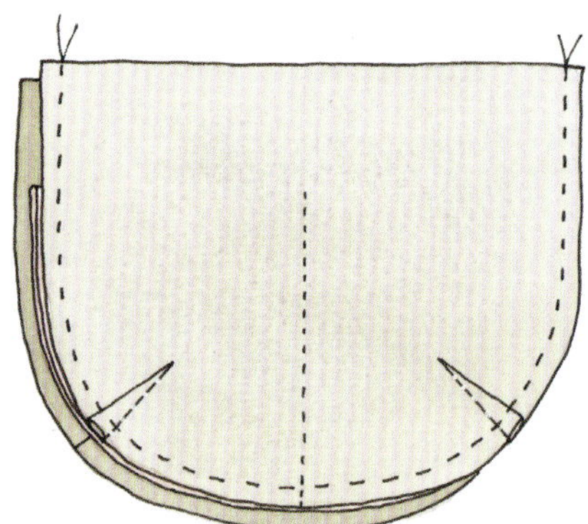

4 Take the front and back main fabric pieces for the body of the bag and, with right sides together, pin and sew a ⅜in (1cm) seam around the outer edge. Take care to line up the dart seams and to capture the pocket edges within the seam.

5 To make up the flap, with right sides together, sew the printed main fabric to the lining with a ⅜in (1cm) seam around the outer edge. Leave the straight top edge open. Clip the corners (see page 112), turn right side out, and press. Topstitch the edges of the flap to finish. Now sew the main pouch lining pieces together in the same way as you did the main bag. Trim all of the curved edges (see page 112).

6 To make up the strap, you first need to decide how you would like it to look— for fabric handles, make up a long main fabric strip, 2in (5cm) wide. To do this, first cut a strip 3½in (9cm) wide, press, and fold and sew the edges to create a neat strip. If you are going to use leather braids like the ones shown here, cut a long strip of leather. If you don't have leather strips you can make long strips by cutting a spiral from a smaller scrap. Try to cut as evenly as possible, but with some rough edges—it looks good for this strap.

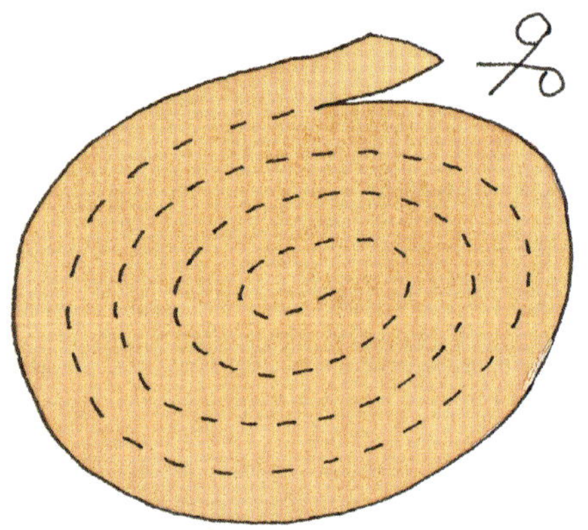

7 To braid the leather, with three strips, machine sew one end about 2½in (6cm) in (if your machine is strong enough to do so, if not, tie the ends), and then tightly braid the strips to the length of strap you want. To secure, sew or tie closed leaving 2½in (6cm) free at the end.

8 You will need to make small tabs to poke out of the bag to which you can tie the straps. Use leather or fabric to do this—cut a strip of your chosen material as wide as the D-rings you are going to use and 6in (15cm) long. Thread the strip through the D-ring and sew at the base to secure. Make two tabs in total, one for each end of the strap. The tabs are attached when the top seam of the bag is sewn.

9 You can now finish making up the bag. This is done using the "pull-through" method. With the main pouch still right side facing in, tuck the handle tab ends into the sides, pointing down into the bag and pin them in place. With the lining pouch turned right side facing out, insert it into the main bag and pin it in place around the top edge of the bag. Sew a ⅜in (1cm) seam around the front and sides of the bag, securing the handle tabs in place. Leave an opening of 10in (25cm) along the back edge for turning and attaching the flap.

10 Turn the whole bag right side out and press the top edge. Insert the flap into the 10in (25cm) opening, pin, and sew a neat seam all around the top edge of the bag, securing the flap, closing the opening, and neatly finishing the top edge. To finish, tie or stitch the strap to the D-rings depending on the style of strap you have chosen.

diaper bag

This bag just what you need to take the little one out for the day, with plenty of room inside for diapers and changes of clothes—there's also a matching changing mat. The print is a rainy day design, but you could choose a pattern to complement your stroller if you wanted to.

skill level: ●●●

printing technique

stencil (see page 12) and eraser stamp (see page 10)

materials

Main fabric

Front and back panels: cut two, 16 x 11in (41 x 28cm)

Sides: cut two, 4 x 11in (10 x 28cm)

Base: cut one, 16 x 4in (41 x 10cm)

Bellows pockets: cut two, 10 x 8in (25 x 20cm)

Handle strip: cut one, 39 x 4in (1m x 10cm)

Changing mat (optional): cut one, 24 x 14in (60 x 35cm)

Waterproof lining fabric

Front and back panels: cut two, 16 x 11in (41 x 28cm)

Sides: cut two, 4 x 11in (10 x 28cm)

Base: cut one, 16 x 4in (41 x 10cm)

Bellows pockets: cut two, 10 x 8in (25 x 20cm)

Inside pocket pieces: cut two, 16 x 8in (41 x 20cm)

Zipper edging: cut two, 14 x 2½in (36 x 6cm)

Iron-on interfacing

Front and back panels: cut two, 16 x 11in (41 x 28cm)

Sides: cut two, 4 x 11in (10 x 28cm)

Base: cut one, 16 x 4in (41 x 10cm)

Bellows pockets: cut two, 10 x 8in (25 x 20cm)

Two magnetic closures

1½in (40mm) D-ring and tribar slide (strap adjuster)

Matching thread

Matching zipper

Toweling, 24 x 14in (60 x 35cm) (optional)

printing tools

Freezer paper or contact paper

Small eraser

Sharp knife

Lino cutters

Fabric paint

Sponges

1 The main print on this fabric is made with stencil, and an eraser stamp is then used to add raindrops. You will need to draw a basic cloud shape at 2 x 4in (5 x 10cm) and a raindrop that is ¾in (2cm) wide. Prepare your stencil and carved eraser stamp as described on pages 10 and 12. Then, cut out your main fabric pattern pieces slightly larger than you need, press, and then print your fabric. Allow the fabric to dry completely before ironing at a high temperature to set the fabric paint.

2 Cut out your fabric to the exact pattern sizes and iron the interfacing onto all of the main fabric pieces.

3 The front pockets are bellows pockets with magnetic closings (see page 114). Working with one piece of main fabric and one lining piece, with right sides together, sew the top seam of the pocket pieces, turn right side out, and press the top edge. Find and mark the center of the top edge of the pockets and, on the lining side, attach the thinner part of the magnetic closing, about ⅜in (1cm) down from the top edge. Do this on both pockets.

4 Lay the pockets flat with right sides down, fold both sides in on themselves by 1in (2.5cm) and press. Now fold the folded part back on itself and press again, so you have an accordion effect on each side.

5 Find and mark the center of the front main fabric piece. Place the pockets, lining side down, in the center with their bottom edges aligned. You will need to fold the accordion sides flat to sew the pocket seams to the main fabric. Pin the sides to the main fabric, where they'll naturally lay when the accordion is folded up, and sew in place. The pockets should lay flat when you have finished. Mark the positions of the magnetic closures by pressing the front pockets into the main fabric to leave an indent. Attach the thickest half of the magnetic closure through the main fabric and open out the arms at the back.

6 To attach the base of the bag to the front panel, with right sides together, sew a ⅜in (1cm) seam (see page 110) leaving ⅜in (1cm) gaps at each end. Make sure that you capture the bottom of the pockets in the seam. Reverse stitch over the central seams a few times for extra strength. Sew the back panel and the sides of the main fabric to the base in the same way. Sew the side seams with a ⅜in (1cm) seam, creating the main bag pouch.

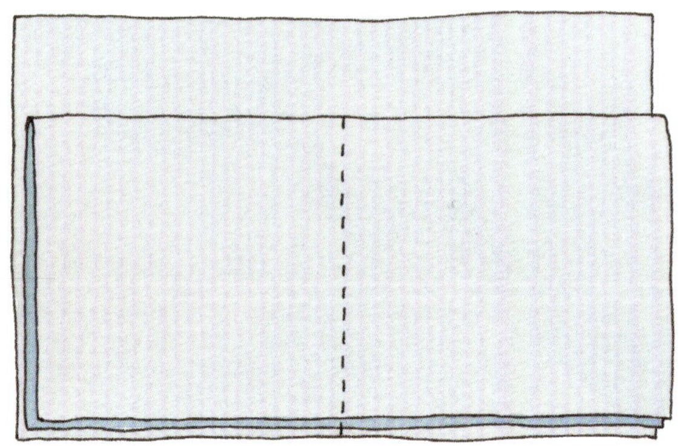

7 To make the internal pockets, fold and press the inside pocket pieces in half and place one each to the lining front and back pieces. Pin them in place and sew the dividing seams where you want them (one seam will give you two pockets, two seams will give you three pockets).

8 To make up the lining, sew the base piece to the front and back pieces with ⅜in (1cm) seams, capturing the pockets pieces and leaving a ⅜in (1cm) gap at each end. Then sew the sidepieces to the base and close all of the side seams.

9 To house the zipper, fold and press a ⅜in (1cm) hem around the zipper-edging piece, fold the whole thing in half, and press. Pin and sew along the edge of the zipper leaving the zipper long at each end. Make small tabs to cover the zipper ends and sew in place with squares of stitches.

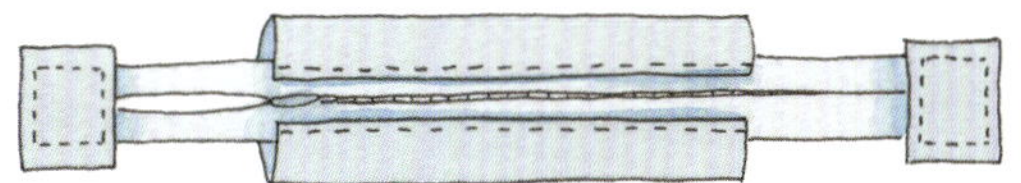

10 Attach the zipper to the lining by sewing it to the right side of the fabric, 1½in (4cm) down from the top edge on either side.

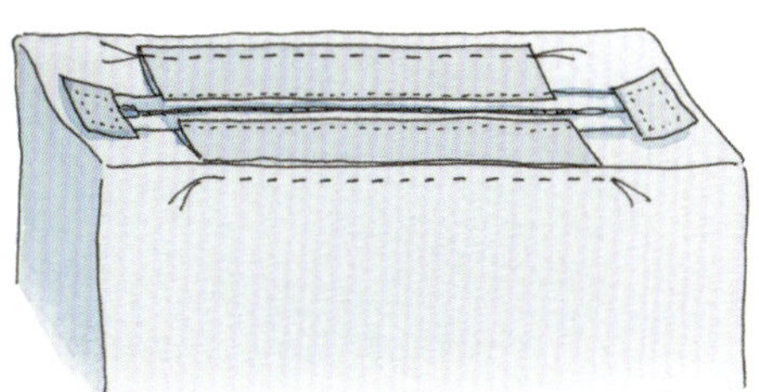

11 To make the handles, fold and press a ⅜in (1cm) hem along both edges of the handle strip and sew a neat edge down both sides. Cut off a 6in (15cm) length to use with the D-ring and leave the rest to attach to the strap adjuster.

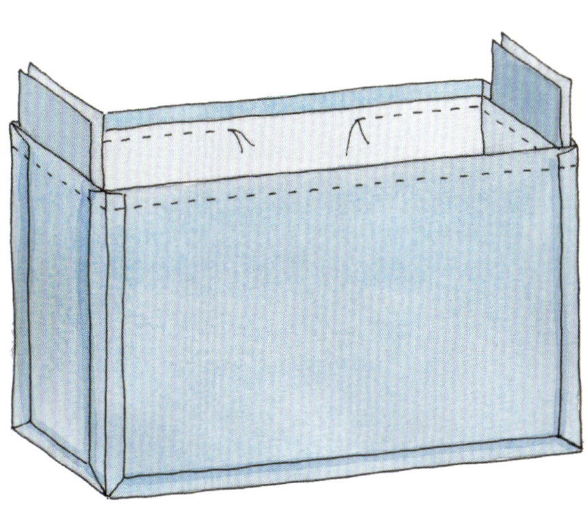

12 The bag is made up using the "pull through" method. The whole bag is made up inside out and then pulled through an opening to finish. With the main bag pouch inside out, turn the lining right side out and insert it into the main bag. Pin it in place all around the top edge of the main bag. At each side, insert the handle tab and strip between the lining fabric and the main fabric. The handles should face down toward the bottom of the bag. Sew a ⅜in (1cm) seam all around the top edge securing the handles and the lining at the same time. Leave a 4in (10cm) opening on the back edge to allow for turning.

13 Pull the whole bag through the opening, press the top edge, and sew a neat seam all around the top to close the opening.

14 If you want to make the matching changing mat, print the main fabric to match the bag and, with right sides together, sew the main fabric and the toweling together all around the outer edge, leaving just a small opening. Trim the corners (see page 112) and pull through the opening. Press the edges and sew a neat edge seam to close the opening and finish.

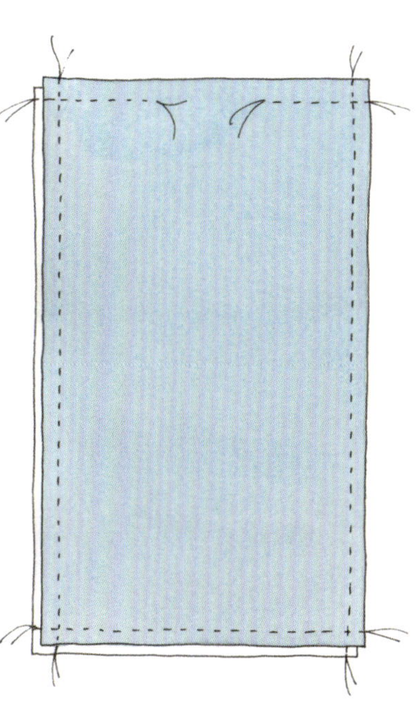

CHAPTER 3

other printing methods

ceramic decal printing

Transform plain ceramic items into your own stunning designer pieces using your inkjet printer and the very clever inkjet decal paper.

skill level: ●●●

printing technique
ceramic transfer (see page 16)

materials

Feather print motifs on page 120
Ceramic item

printing tools

Letter-sized (A4) inkjet decal paper
Clear spray varnish
Hairdryer
Scissors or craft knife

PRINTING TIPS

This technique has endless possibilities as you can use any artwork you like. Use your computer's graphics/photo program to prepare your images and print them to scale on the special paper. You don't need to reverse the image.

1 Your finished ceramic item will be fairly durable but cannot go in a dishwasher and will not survive too much scrubbing. Decorate something like a vase or a storage jar that will not require much washing. Scale up the motifs on page 120 to the sizes you need for your ceramic item and print them onto the shiny side of your inkjet decal paper, as described on page 16.

2 Once the ink is dry, spray the paper with a thin, even coat of clear varnish. Use a hairdryer to dry the varnish, then repeat to add two more thin coats. The varnish will protect your ink from running when you place your decal in water in step 5.

3 When the varnish is completely dry, cut out the decals using scissors or a craft knife. Leave the narrowest border possible.

4 Place each decal in turn in a bowl of water and leave for 30 seconds until you can feel the backing paper starting to slide off.

5 Remove from the water with the backing paper still attached, and place it on your ceramic item. Smooth the decal down while gently sliding out the backing paper. Smooth over the decal with your finger to remove any air bubbles. Repeat with the remaining decals.

6 Preheat your oven to 130ºC/250ºF/ Gas ½ and place your ceramic item on the middle shelf. Leave it there to dry for 10–15 minutes, then remove and leave to cool.

simple coin purse

This simple lined purse is a good introduction to working with linings and zippers; once you've mastered them you can attempt many more complicated projects. The print design for this purse is made on the computer, layering images together, then printed out onto photo-transfer paper and ironed onto your fabric.

skill level: ●●●

printing technique
photo transfer (see page 15)

materials

Postcard image on page 126

Main fabric
Cut two, 8 x 6in (20 x 15cm)

Lining fabric
Cut two, 8 x 6in (20 x 15cm)

Matching zipper, 6in (15cm)
Matching thread

printing tools

Iron-on photo-transfer paper
Inkjet printer
Iron
Scissors

1 Prepare your photo-transfer print as described on page 15. Then, cut out your fabric slightly larger than your transfer image and iron it before you attach the transfer. Iron the transfer image onto the fabric according to the manufacturer's instructions and remove the backing paper. Take care not to apply direct heat to the image throughout the rest of the making process.

2 To attach the zipper, change to the zipper foot on your sewing machine, place the zipper face down along a top edge of the main fabric, and sew in place with a neat seam along the edge (see page 113). Line up the zipper with the other top edge and sew in place in the same way.

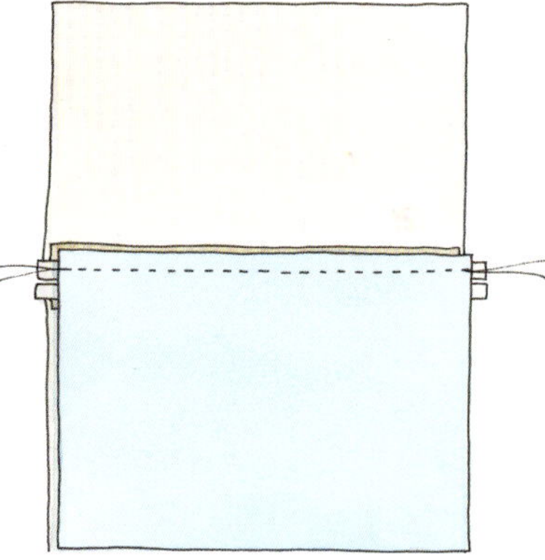

3 To attach the lining, repeat the previous step but on the other side of the zipper. Lay your main fabric flat on its back with the zipper in the center and press flat (be careful with your photo transfer—keep it cool and only apply light pressure). Match one piece of lining fabric to the top edge of the zipper, so it is covering the zipper, pin, and sew a neat seam following the same line of stitches as for the main fabric. Repeat this on the other side with the other piece of lining fabric. Lay the whole purse out flat and press the zipper edges.

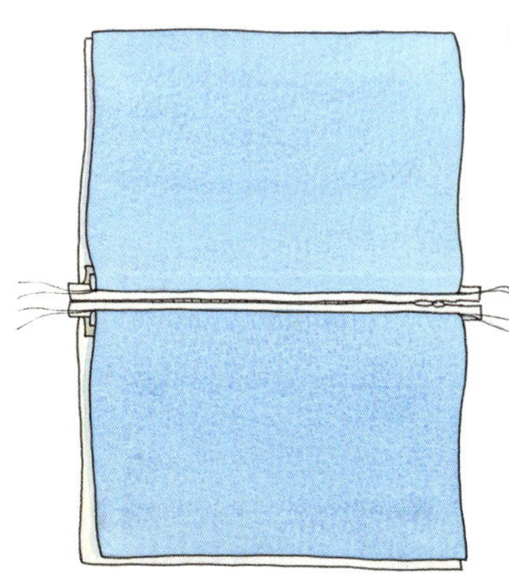

4 Open out the fabric matching the edges of the lining and the main fabric pieces right sides together. With the zipper concealed in the center, sew a ⅜in (1cm) seam all around the outer edges (see page 110), leaving a 2in (5cm) gap on the bottom edge of the lining for turning.

5 Trim the corners (see page 112) and pull the whole purse through the opening in the lining, turning it right side out. Sew the opening in the lining closed, and then push the lining inside the purse.

Women Artists

photo patchwork quilt

You can make a memory quilt from old family photos or from images of special places you have visited. Pick images with similar coloring or use your computer to adjust them. Match the rest of your patchwork pieces to this color theme.

skill level: ●●

printing technique

photo transfer (see page 15)

materials

Fabric: (white or cream cotton fabric), you will need approx. 40 x 40in (102 x 102cm) in total for the front:

Cut 16 photo squares, 6 x 6in (15 x 15cm)

Cut 4 quilt edging strips, 32½ x 2½in (82 x 6cm)

Sufficient fabric to make 32 printed side strips and 16 corner squares (see instructions)

Backing fabric: 32½ x 32½in (82 x 82cm)

Scissors, pins, needle, matching thread, tape measure

printing tools

Computer

Inkjet printer

Letter-sized (A4) sheets of Inkjet photo transfer paper: 8+

1 For this project you will need 16 photographic images. You can use the photo-editing software on your computer to adjust the color and size of your images. Each one must be 5½ x 5½in (14 x 14cm). Use your computer to reverse the images, then print them on inkjet photo transfer paper, as described on page 15. The images will be the right way around when you transfer them to the fabric.

2 Cut out the 16 photo squares from your fabric and iron them flat. Cut out each printed image, leaving a ½in (1cm) border of photo transfer paper around each one.

3 Place a paper image face down on a fabric square and, following the instructions that came with your photo transfer paper, iron your transfer in place and peel away the backing. Repeat to make 16 fabric photo squares.

PRINTING TIPS

Photo transfers will print back to front, so remember to reverse your images before transferring them to the fabric. Take care when ironing the seams as the photo transfers do not like direct heat.

4 Each photo square on the quilt is surrounded by pieces of printed fabric. For these, either use printed offcuts from other projects or print pieces of fabric specially using any technique you like from this book. Either way, you must end up with 32 printed side strips, each measuring 2½ x 6in (6 x 15cm) and 16 corner squares, each measuring 2½ x 2½in (6 x 6cm). Iron all your fabric to make it easier to line up the edges when constructing the quilt.

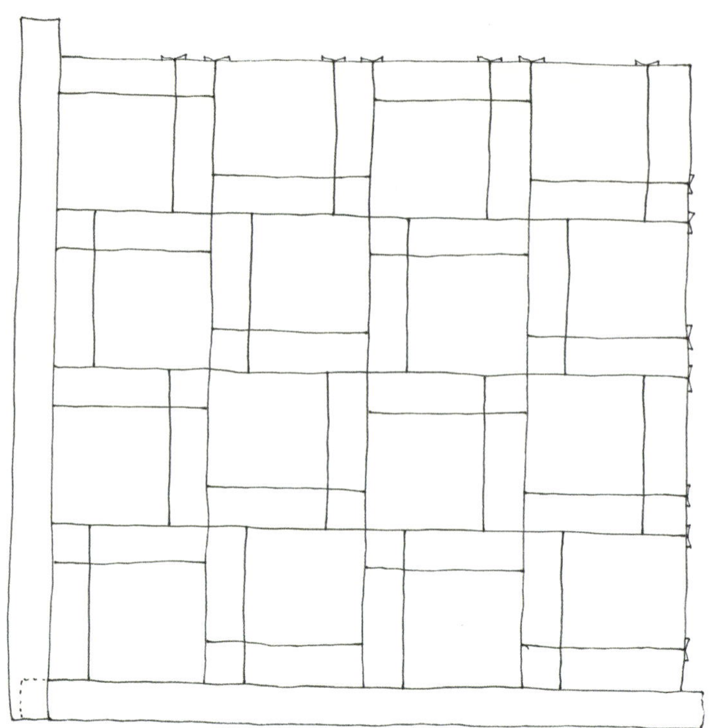

5 When sewing the quilt together, think of it as 16 large squares, each made up of four pieces—the photo square, two side strips and a corner square.

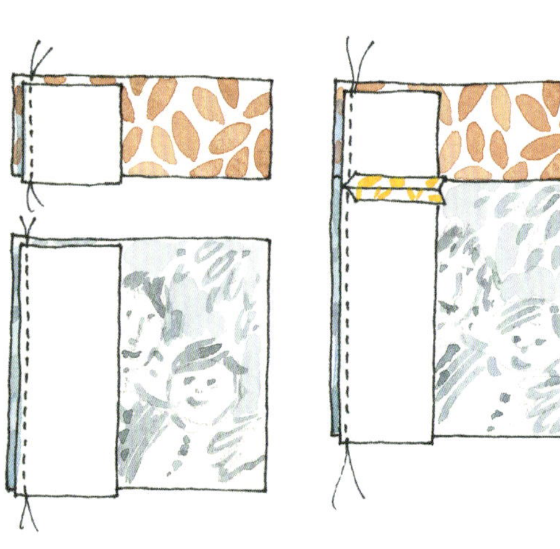

6 Leaving a ½in (1cm) seam allowance (see page 110), first join a corner square to a side strip and a side strip to the photo square. Finally, join the corner square with its side strip to the photo square with its side strip. Follow the illustration to check how to make up the large squares.

7 Press all the seams open on the wrong side as you work (see page 110), taking care not to iron directly on the photo-transfers as ironing will damage them.

8 Once all 16 large squares are ready, sew them together in rows to make four strips, each consisting of four squares. Again, leave a ½in (1cm) seam allowance and press all the seams open on the wrong side.

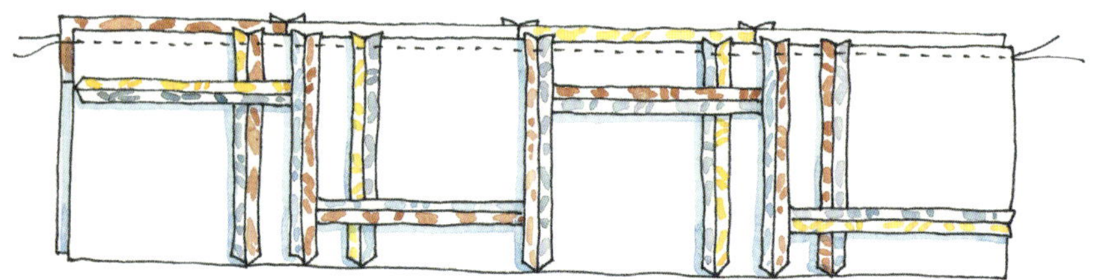

9 Now join the four strips together to make one big panel. Once again, leave a ½in (1cm) seam allowance and press all the seams open on the wrong side.

10 To finish your quilt, sew an edging strip to each side. Position the first strip along one side, right side to right side, leaving ½in (1cm) spare at the top and a 2in (5cm) overhang at the bottom. Sew them together leaving a ½in (1cm) seam allowance. When you join the next strip, attach it to the 2in (5cm) overhang to create a neat, square corner.

11 Continue adding edging strips in this way until you have a square quilt measuring 32½ x 32½in (82 x 82cm). Press all the seams open on the wrong side.

12 To attach the backing fabric, lay it on top of the quilt, right side to right side. Pin it in place. Leaving a ½in (1cm) seam allowance, sew around all four sides. Leave a small opening in one edge for turning.

13 Trim the corners (see page 112) and turn the quilt to the right side through the opening. Push out all the corners from the inside and press the edges. Hand-sew the opening closed, then topstitch (see page 112) a neat line of stitches all the way around to finish the quilt.

PRINTING TIPS

For the printed panels of fabric, try to stick to two or three colors that complement each other, or you can really get creative and use as many colors as you like!

zipprered wallet

This is such a versatile wallet; it could be used to hold coins and cards, or it would make a handy case for sewing needles and threads. A real fern leaf was used for this print; the paint was rollered directly on the leaf and then the leaf pressed onto the fabric.

skill level: ●●●

printing technique
leaf print (see page 16)

materials

Main fabric

Cut one, 8¼ x 7in (21 x 18cm)

Zipper tab ends: cut two, 3½ x 2½in (9 x 6cm)

Lining fabric

Main panel: cut one, 8¼ x 7in (21 x 18cm)

Pocket pieces: cut two, 7 x 6in (18 x 15cm)

Small pocket pieces: cut two, 7 x 5in (18 x 13cm)

Zipper, 18in (45cm)

Bias binding, 3ft (1m)

Iron-on interfacing

Matching thread

printing tools

Fern leaf for printing

Sponge roller

Fabric paint

Brayer or rolling pin

1 Cut out all of the pattern pieces in the main and lining fabrics, making sure to add curved corners—you can do this by using a compass or drawing around a plate edge, as long as they all match it doesn't matter what size or shape you use. Then, print the fabric with your leaves, as described on page 16. Once your design is complete, allow the fabric to dry before ironing it on a high heat to set the fabric paint.

2 Iron the interfacing onto the main fabric to give it more structure. Now, press the pocket fabric pieces in half, layer onto the right side of the lining fabric, pin in place, and sew dividing seams where you want them.

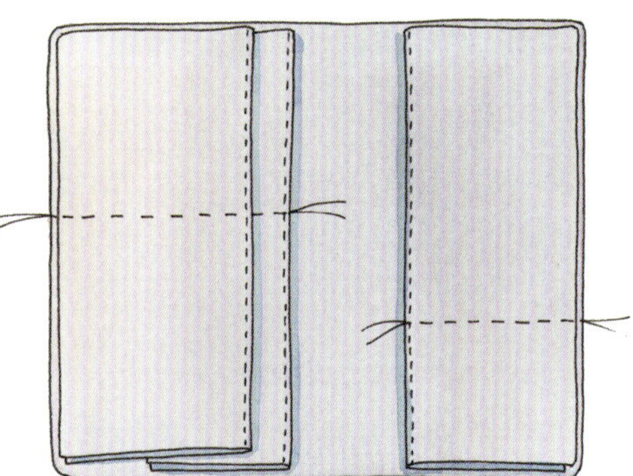

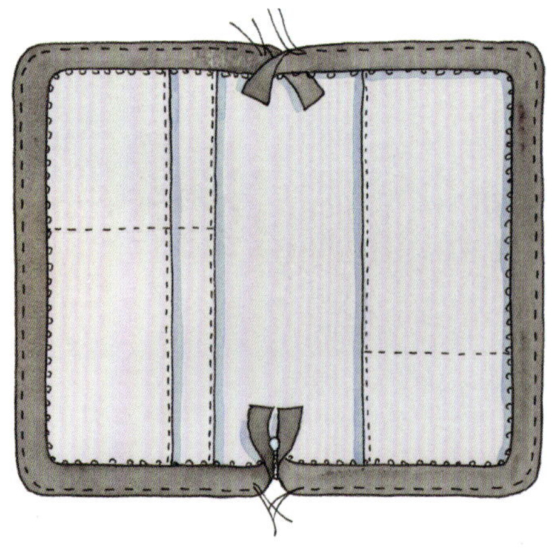

3 Pin the lining fabric to the main fabric wrong sides together, and begin to attach the zipper. Open the zipper fully, then find and mark the center of the purse at both side edges, this is where your zipper will begin and end. Pin the zipper in place around all sides, meeting at the other side and leaving a long end on the zipper to cover later. It's important that the zipper isn't twisted or laying unevenly—test the zipper by closing it while it is just pinned to see if everything lines up correctly. When you are happy, sew the zipper in place all around the outer edge.

4 Sew bias binding all around the purse to house any raw edges (see page 113). Start near the end of the zipper and make sure to pull it tight around the corners.

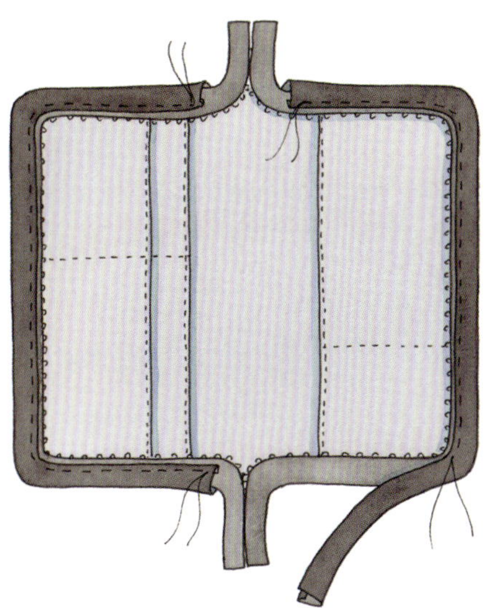

5 Finally, add covers to the zipper ends. Take your strips of main fabric and fold with the right sides together, sew the top and one side of the tab, trim corners (see page 112), and turn right side out. Fold under the raw ends and press. Slot the cover over the zipper end, pin in place, then sew a square of stitches to secure.

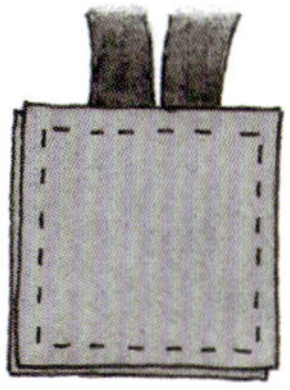

mini tote bag

This simple little bag is a perfect miniature of Mommy's tote bag, and could have so many uses. Photos of vintage fabric have been turned into iron-on transfers to create this cute bunting design.

skill level: ●●●

printing technique
photo transfer (see page 15)

materials

Bunting images on page 126

Main fabric

Front and back: cut two, 16 x 18in (40 x 45cm)

Handle strips: cut two, 2½ x 8in (6 x 20cm)

Matching thread

printing tools

Photo-transfer paper

Inkjet printer

Image program

Iron

1 Cut out the main fabric and press to prepare for printing. Prepare your photo-transfer print as described on page 15. Be careful with your design once you have peeled the backing paper off—do not iron directly onto the transfer.

2 First, make up the handles. Fold and press ⅜in (1cm) hems on both sides of the handle strips, fold, and press in half matching up the edges. Topstitch (see page 112) a neat seam down both sides to finish.

3 To make up the main body of the bag, French seams are used so that all raw edges will be hidden (see page 111). Take your two main pieces of fabric and place them wrong sides together. Sew a ⅜in (1cm) seam around the two sides and base (see page 110).

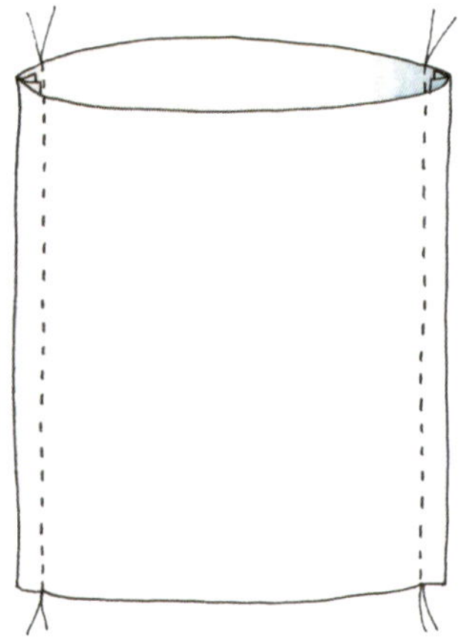

4 Trim the seam edge down so that it is as narrow as you can make it without compromising the stitches. Turn the whole bag inside out and press the seams. Sew another ⅜in (1cm) seam around the edges and base enclosing all the raw edges inside. Turn right side out and press again.

5 Hem the top edge of the bag and attach the handles at the same time. Fold the top edge inward and press a ⅜in (1cm) hem around the top, then fold another hem, about 1¼in (3cm), enclosing the first hem inside (see page 111). Take your handles and tuck them into the hem to hide the raw ends, pin in place, and sew all around the base of the hem securing the handles and closing the hem seam. Now sew another line of stitches all around the very top of the edge to finish.

sewing techniques

All the projects in this book are designed to be easy to achieve, no matter what your sewing skills. All the equipment used in this book is standard sewing equipment—if you own a sewing machine and have done a little sewing before, chances are that you own everything you need already. If there is a technique or stage you are unsure about, try it out on scrap fabric first so that you don't damage your newly printed fabric by having to unpick several times.

basic equipment

- Sewing machine and zipper foot
- Sharp fabric scissors
- Seam ripper
- Pins
- Safety pins
- Chalk/tailor's chalk
- Tape measure
- Large ruler
- Iron and ironing board

seam allowance

The seam allowance is the distance between a seam and the edge of the fabric. There are many standard measurements for seam allowances but your pattern should always tell you what seam allowance to use. The projects in this book use a ⅜in (1cm) and all the measurements take this seam allowance into account. Occasionally a project might ask you to use a narrower seam allowance, so always read the project text carefully.

simple seam

To sew two pieces of fabric together, line up the fabric with the right sides facing. Pin them together at regular intervals along the edge, then sew a straight line of stitches, following the edge of the fabric. Use the markings on your machine's needle plate to make sure you are sewing straight. Remove the pins as you sew. To turn a corner, insert the needle, raise the presser foot and turn the fabric. Lower the presser foot to continue. When you come to the end of your seam, use the reverse button on your machine and reverse stitch for about ⅜in (1cm) to stop the seam unraveling.

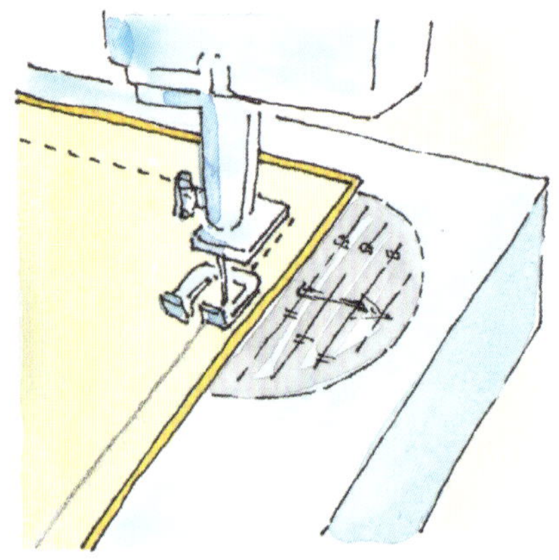

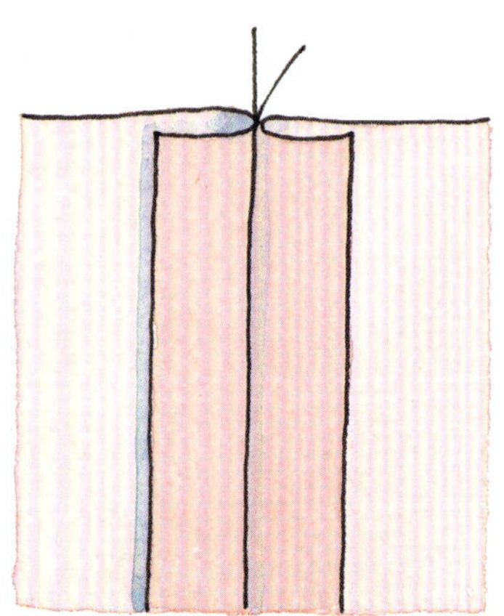

Always press your seams open to get a nice smooth finish.

french seams

These look like a plain seam from the outside but all the raw edges are enclosed inside a small, neat channel inside—very good for unlined items. You work in a slightly different way to a plain seam in that you start with the wrong sides of the fabric facing together and sew a plain ⅜in (1cm) seam all along the edge. The seam is then pressed open and the fabric turned out the other way so that right sides are facing together. Then another ⅜in (1cm) seam is sewn enclosing the raw edges within it.

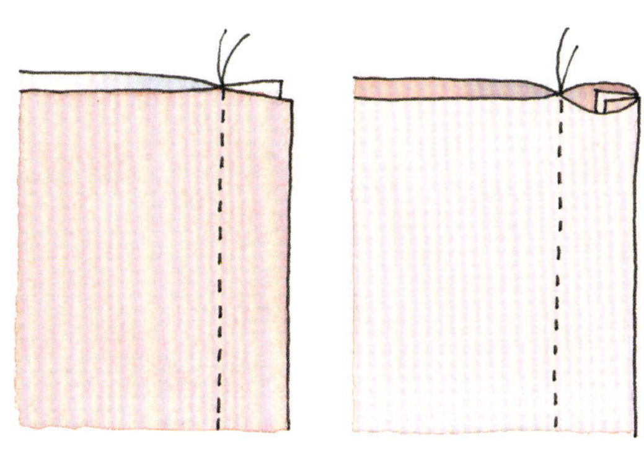

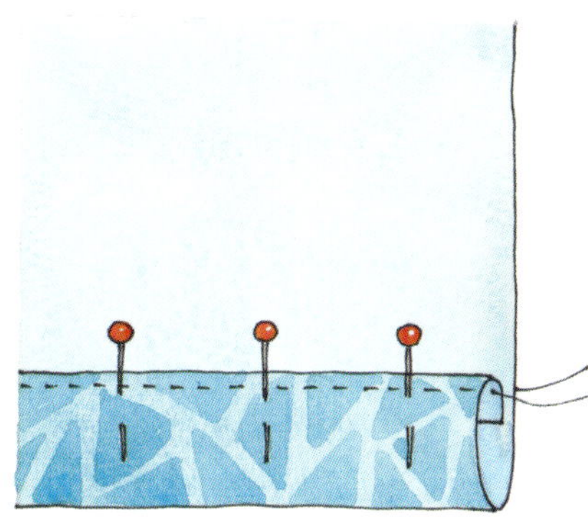

simple hem

All the hems in this book are double hems—hems that completely enclose the raw edges. With the wrong side facing you, fold over the edge of the fabric by 1½in (1cm) along the line where you want your hem to be. Press a crisp edge, then fold the fabric over again by ½in (1cm). Press and pin in place. Sew a neat line of stitches very close to the edge of the second fold, removing the pins as you go.

sewing a neat hemmed corner

This is a simple and effective way to make neat hemmed right-angled corners for projects like napkins or dish towels. The simple folds enclose all the raw edges and reduce the bulky fabric at the corner. This principle works for a seam of any width; just adjust the measurements of the folds as required.

1 With the wrong side facing you, fold and press a ¼in (6mm) hem along both sides of the corner, then turn another ¼in (6mm) hem and press well again. Now unfold the fabric so you can see your foldlines.

2 Next, fold the point of the corner in so it meets the second set of foldlines. Press.

3 Fold a second time across the corner to enclose the raw edges and press again.

4 Now refold your sides along the first ¼in (6mm) foldline and press, then fold again along the second ¼in (6mm) foldline.

5 Your raw edges will all now be enclosed and the ends of the side seams should meet along a neat diagonal line. Sew the sides closed with a neat line of stitches close to the folded edge.

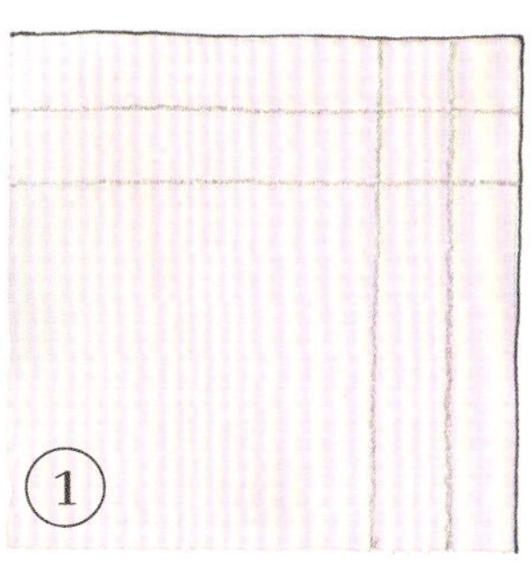

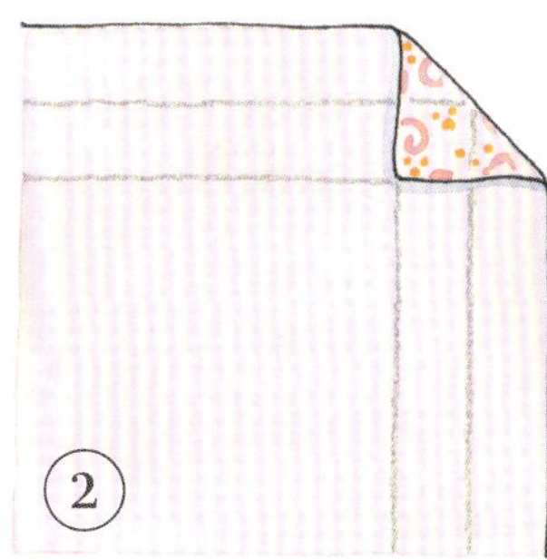

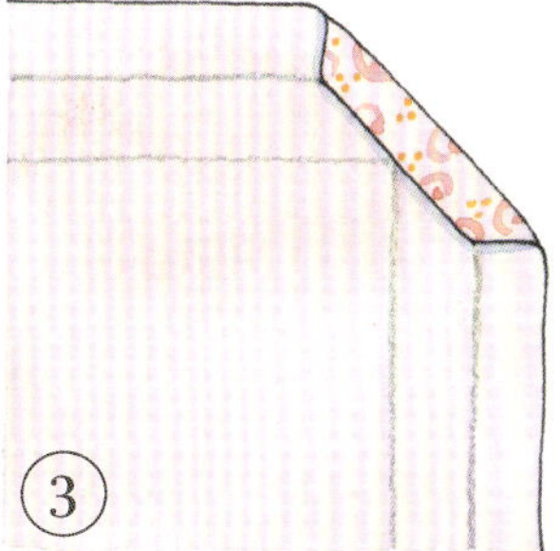

trimming corners and curves

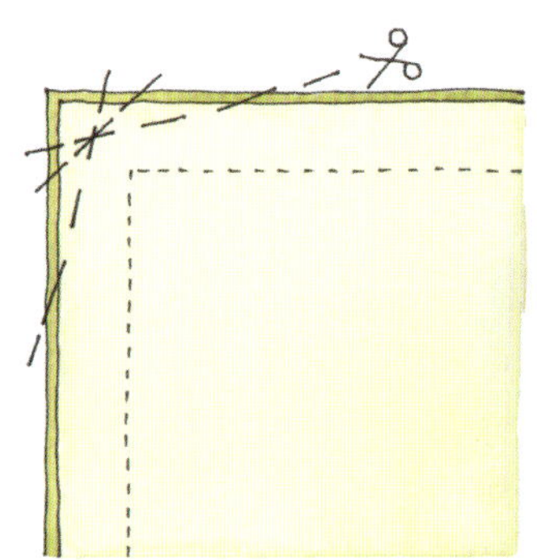

Once you have sewn your seams you need to trim them before you turn your project to the right side. This keeps the seams nice and crisp on the right side. To trim a right-angled corner, cut away the point of the corner on the diagonal, taking care not to cut through the stitches of your seams. When you turn the corner to the right side, it should have a lovely sharp point.

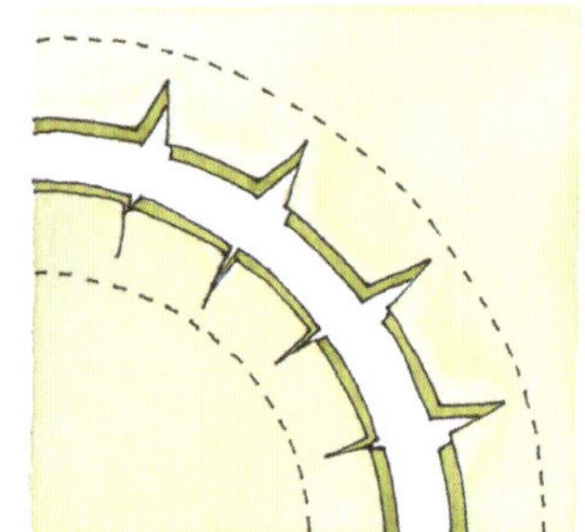

To trim an inside curve, cut away little triangles at regular intervals to reduce the bulk of the fabric, taking care not to cut through the stitches. For an outside curve, make straight cuts to allow the fabric to stretch more easily around the curve. When you turn the curved seam to the right side, it should lie nice and flat, without any wrinkles or puckers.

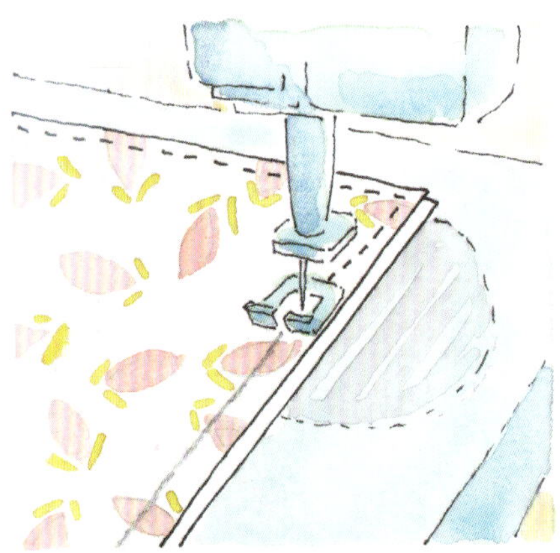

topstitching

This is a decorative stitch that gives a neat finish to a project. You can also use it to close an opening. On the right side, simply sew a neat line of straight stitches very close to the folded edge.

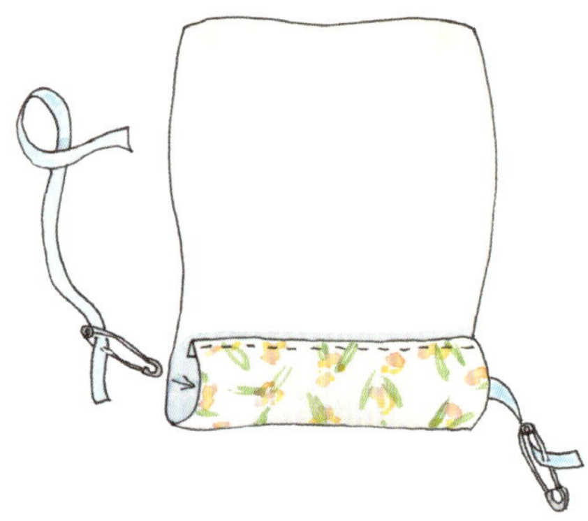

threading cord or elastic through a channel

To thread the end of your cord or elastic through a channel, attach a safety pin to one end of the cord. Insert the pin with the cord attached into one end of the channel. Use the pin to move the cord through the channel, holding onto the pin through the layers of fabric and pushing the pin forward as you pull the fabric backward, out of the way. Be careful not to lose your grip on the pin until it emerges far enough from the other side that you can hold onto the cord comfortably.

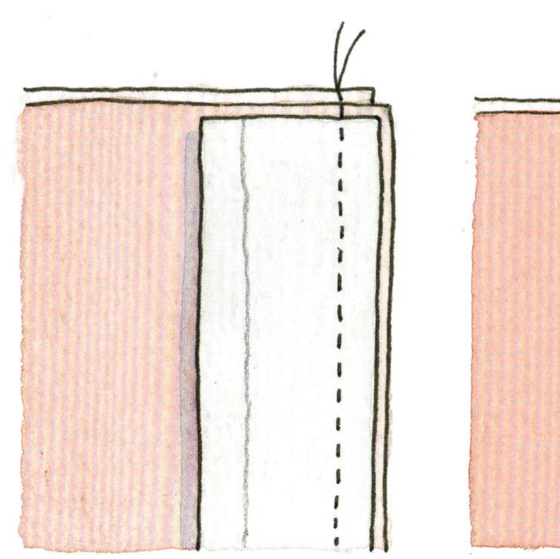

making fabric ties and handles

Making fabric ties or handles is easy. Here are the general principles, but you should adjust all your measurements according to the width of your strip. Start with a strip of fabric twice as wide as you want your finished tie or handle to be, plus ¾in (2cm). With the wrong side facing you, fold over and press a ½in (1cm) hem along both long edges of your strip. Now fold the strip lengthwise, wrong side to wrong side, so the two folded edges meet. Sew together with a neat line of stitches on the right side. Now sew another neat line of stitches along the other long edge of the strip to give you a neat, strong finish.

bias binding edge

This is a neat way to enclose raw edges on the outside of an item. Bias binding strips are available in many colors and widths. Simply pin one raw edge of the binding in place to one edge of the fabric, right sides together, and sew along the fold of the binding to hide stitches. Fold the binding over, enclosing the raw fabric edges of the project, tuck the fold of the binding under, and sew along the other side neatly near the bottom of the binding, to finish.

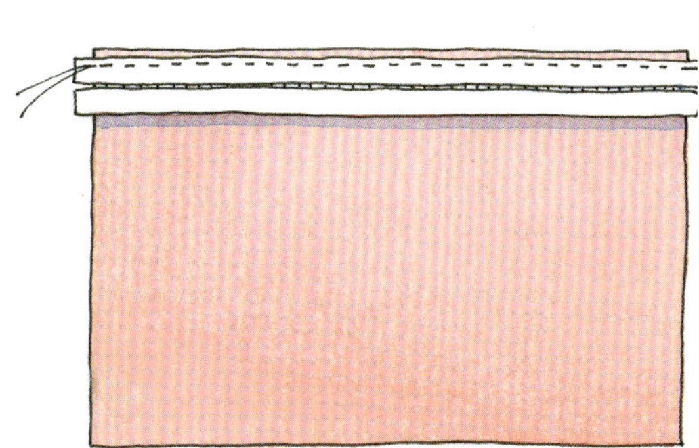

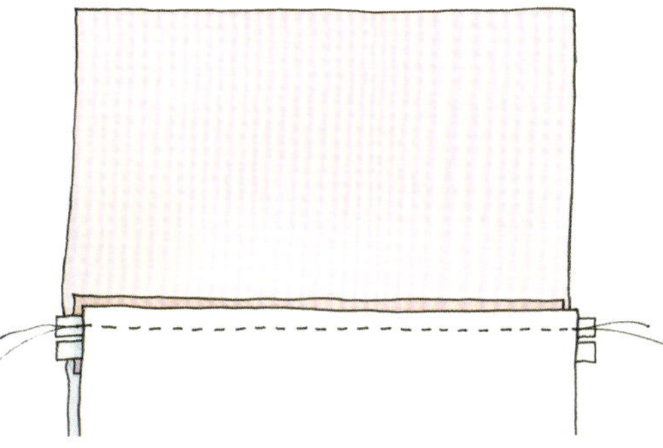

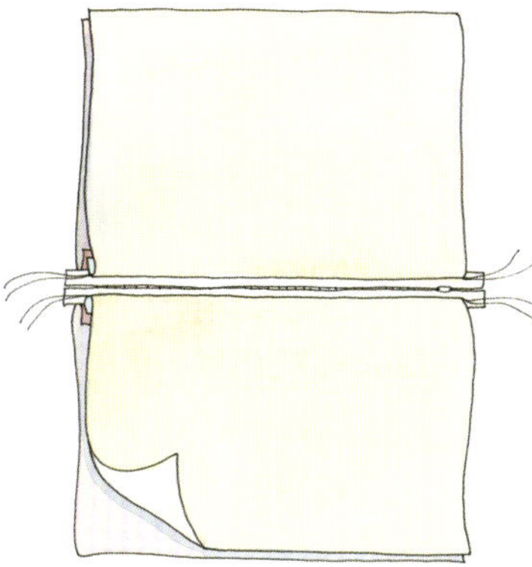

sewing in a zipper

For the projects in this book, zippers are attached to both the lining and main fabrics before making up the bag structure. To do this, change to your zipper foot on your sewing machine, place the zipper face down along a top edge of the main fabric, and sew in place with a neat seam all down the edge. Next, line up the zipper with the other top edge on the main fabric and sew in place in the same way. To attach the lining to the zipper, repeat the previous steps but on the other side of the zipper. Lay your main fabric flat on its back with the zipper in the center and press flat, match one piece of lining fabric to the top edge of the zipper, lay it so that it is covering the zipper, pin, and sew a neat seam following the same line of stitches as used to secure the main fabric in place. Repeat this on the other side, lay out the whole purse flat, and press the zipper edges.

covering a button

If your project calls for a button, why not make a covered one? Two-part metal and plastic self-cover buttons are readily available in a variety of sizes. They consist of a top—the button part—and a back plate. To use, cut out a circle of fabric that is ½in (1cm) wider all around than the button. Hand-sew a line of running stitches around the outer edge of the fabric. Place the fabric, right side up, over the button top, and pull the stitches tight, gathering the fabric around the button as you go. Hold the fabric firmly in place and snap on the button's back plate.

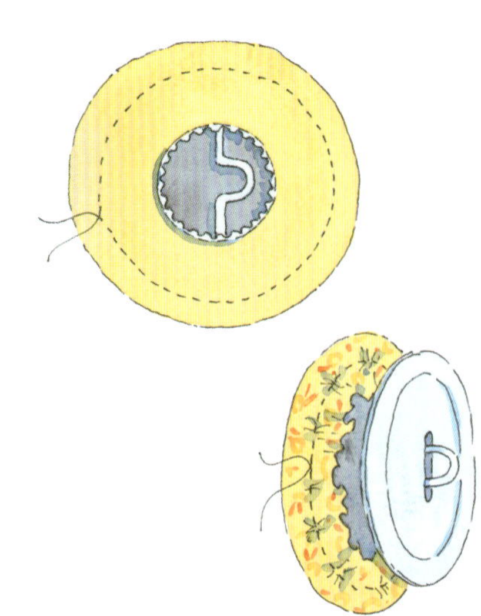

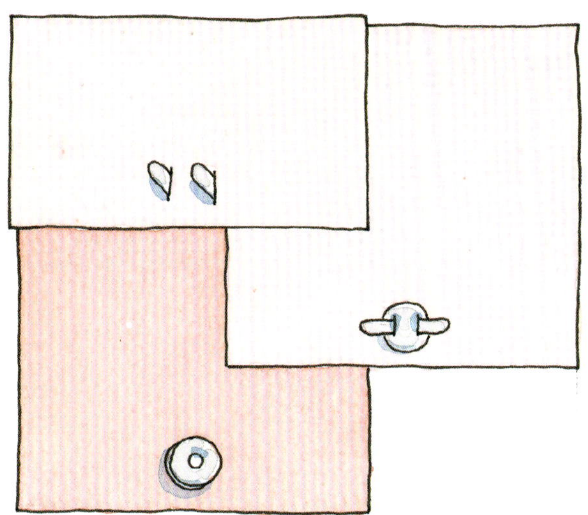

magnetic closings

These are handy little things to master. They are easy to fit but it's worth buying one extra to practice on with scrap fabric the first time you do it, so that you can see and feel how it works. Mark where you want the closing to go and cut two small slits for the arms, push through the fabric, slide over backing plate, and fold out the arms to secure in place. Repeat the process where you want the other side of the closing to go.

print motifs

All of these motifs are printed at half their actual size. They will need to be enlarged to 200% using a photocopier before use.

Honeycomb bunting (page 20)

Tea cozy (page 22)

Quilted oven glove (page 25)

Wall printing (page 28)

Doorstop cube
(page 34)

Leafy lampshade
(page 32)

Envelope clutch
(page 38)

Toiletry bag
(page 36)

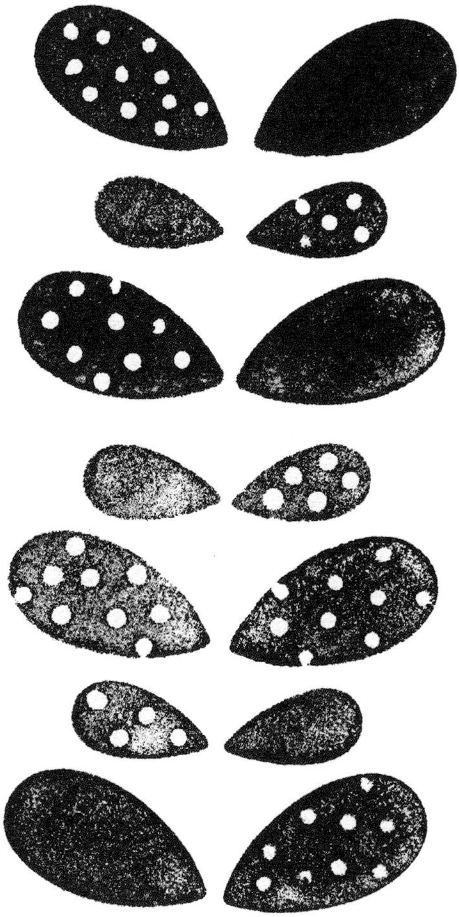

Long satchel
(page 47)

Puffball purse
(page 44)

Children's backpack
(page 30)

Japanese fabric giftwrap
(page 50)

Tie-top curtains
(page 58)

Giant floor pillows
(page 64)

Roll storage
(page 68)

Fern-print coasters
(page 73)

Full-length apron
(page 61)

Gathered purse
(page 76)

Vine-leaf placemat
(page 80)

Table runner
(page 78)

Rounded shoulder bag
(page 89)

Boxy weekender
(page 82)

Simple round pillow
(page 70)

Ceramic decal printing
(page 98)

templates

To use the templates on these pages, most of them first need to be enlarged on a photocopier; all the enlargements are detailed next to each template. Cut out the shape from the photocopy, pin this pattern to your fabric, and cut around it. If the template has a line with two arrows, it is only for half the piece. You need to fold the fabric in half on the straight grain, place that edge of the pattern directly on the fold, and then pin and cut through both layers (but don't cut along the foldline). When you unfold it, you have the complete piece.

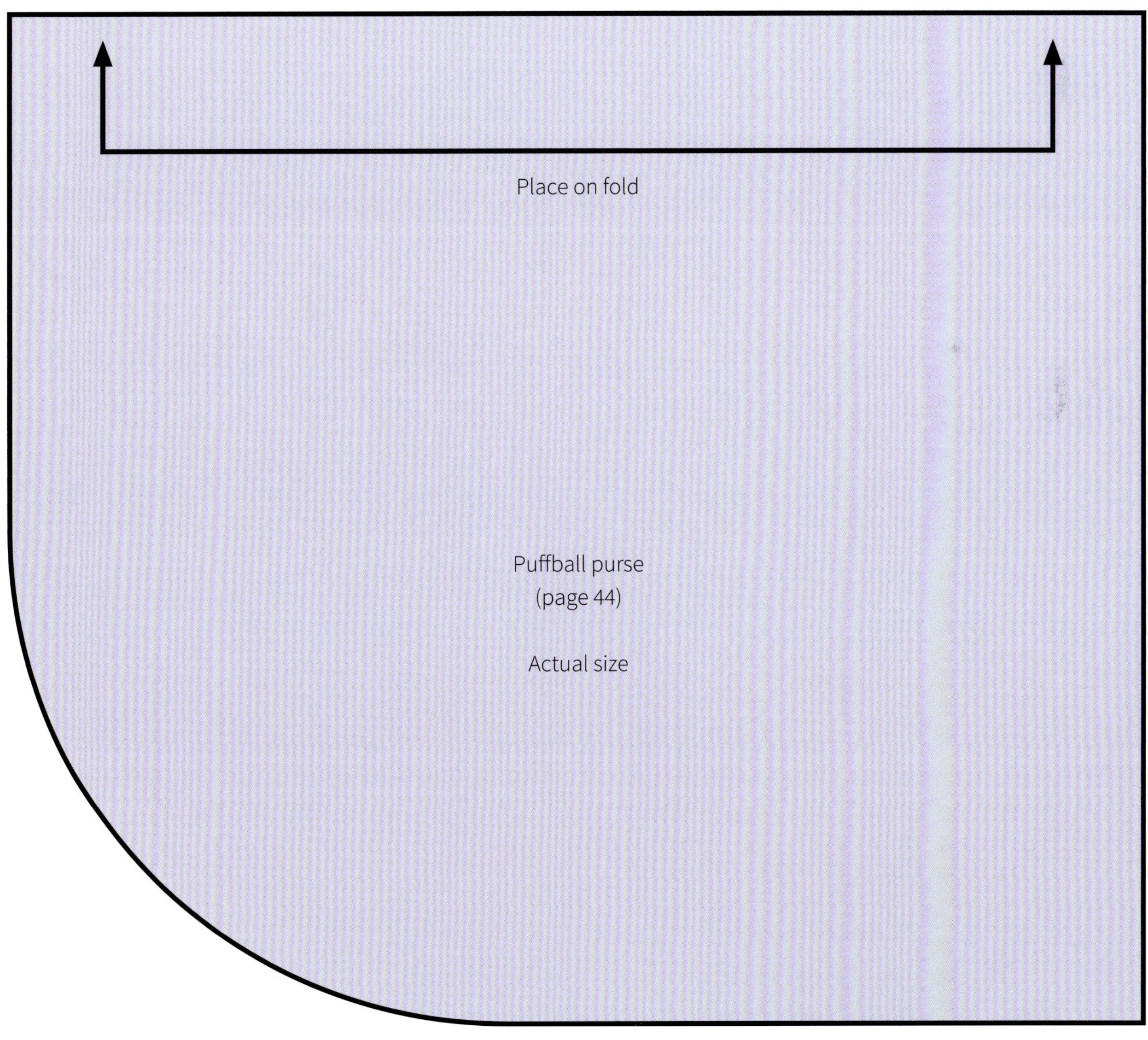

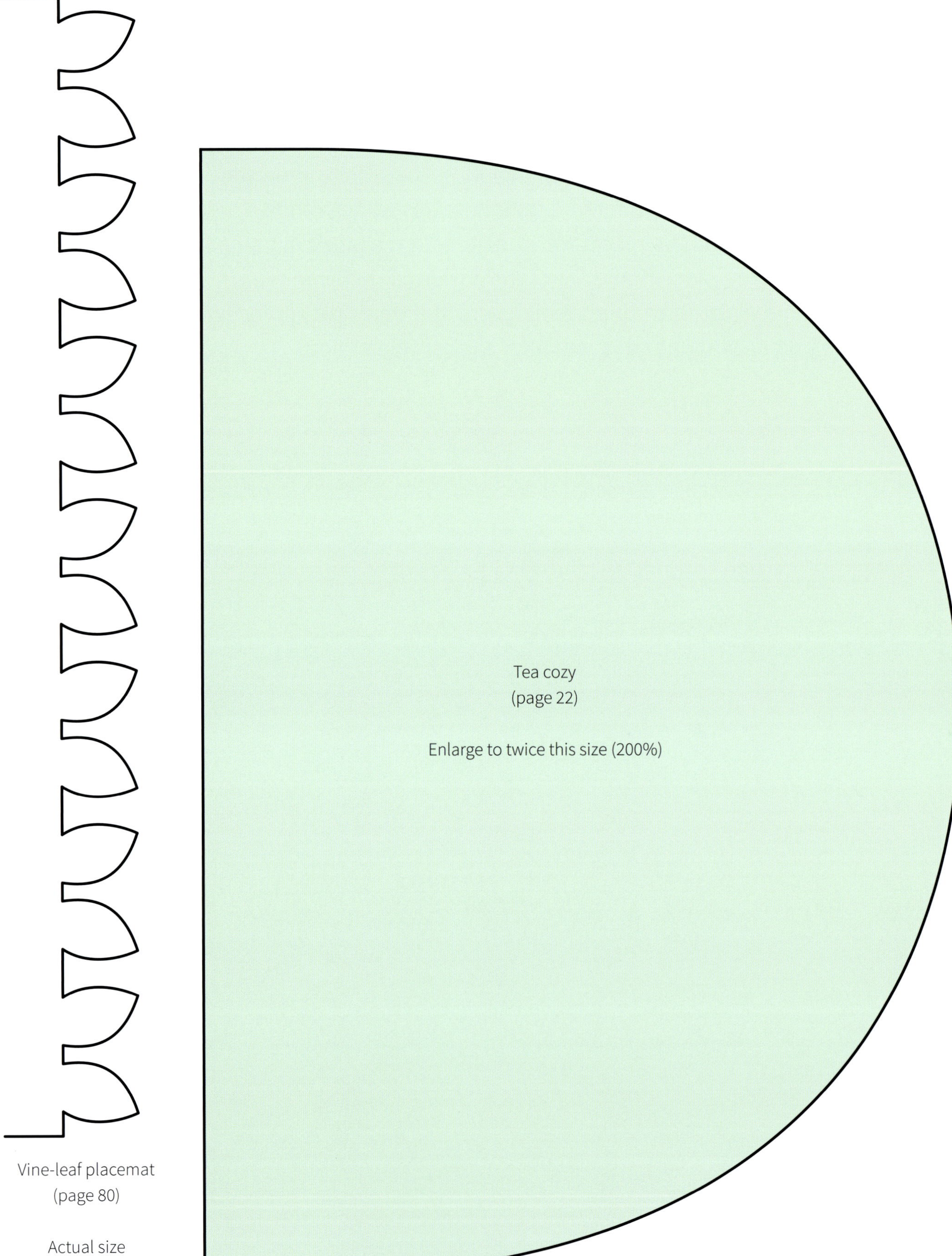

Vine-leaf placemat
(page 80)

Actual size

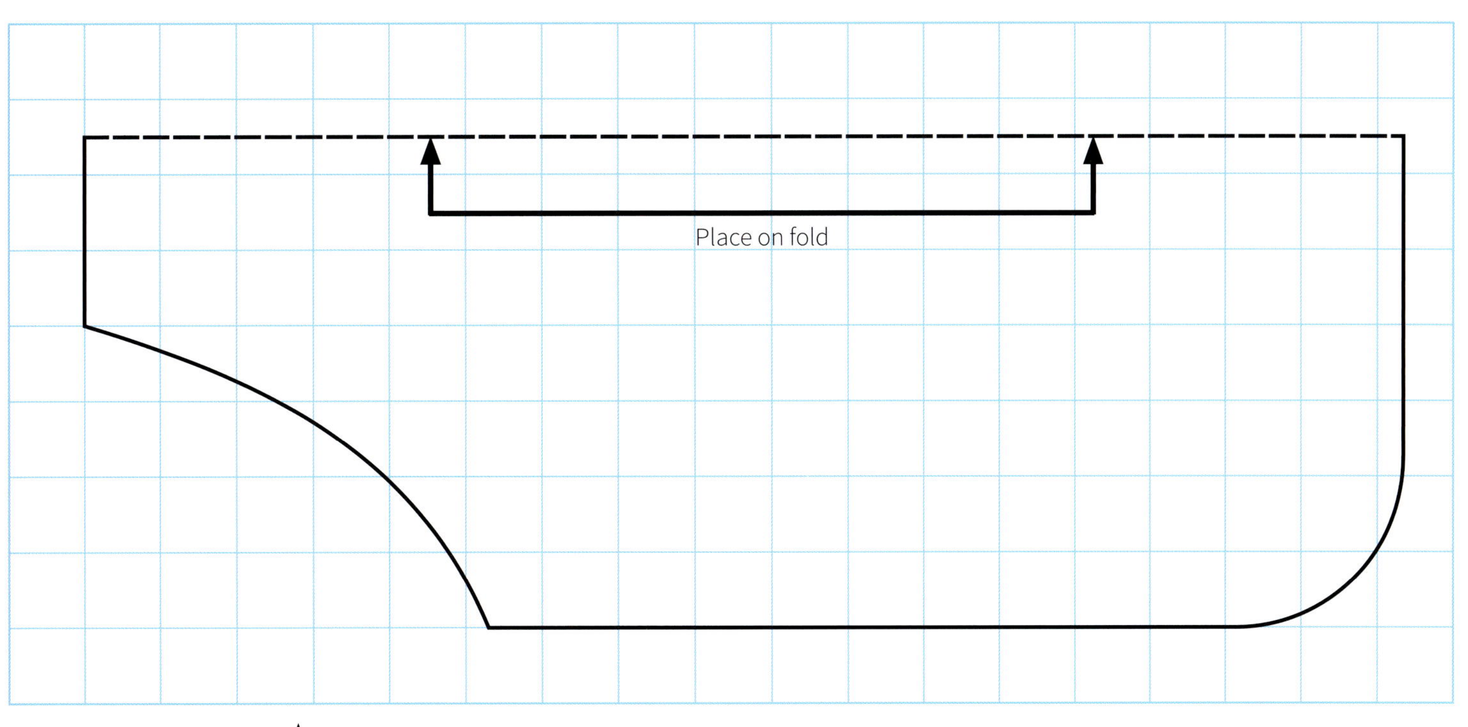

Full-length apron (page 61)
The grid below indicates the size of this template—each square equals 2in (5cm). Draw the apron up to its full size on paper. You may find it easier to use squared pattern paper to do this.

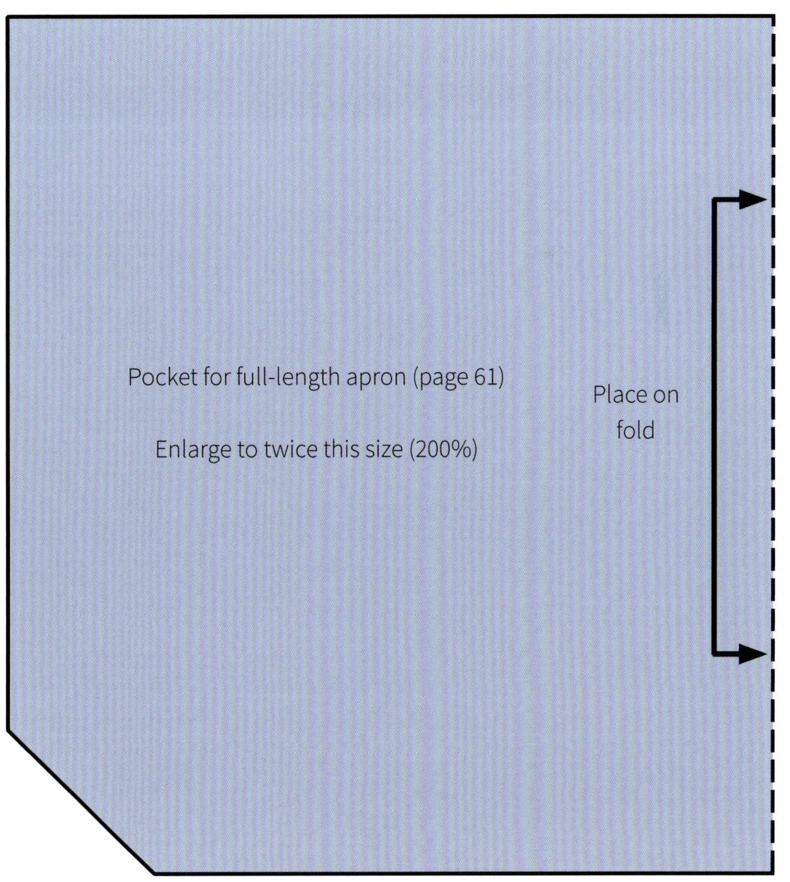

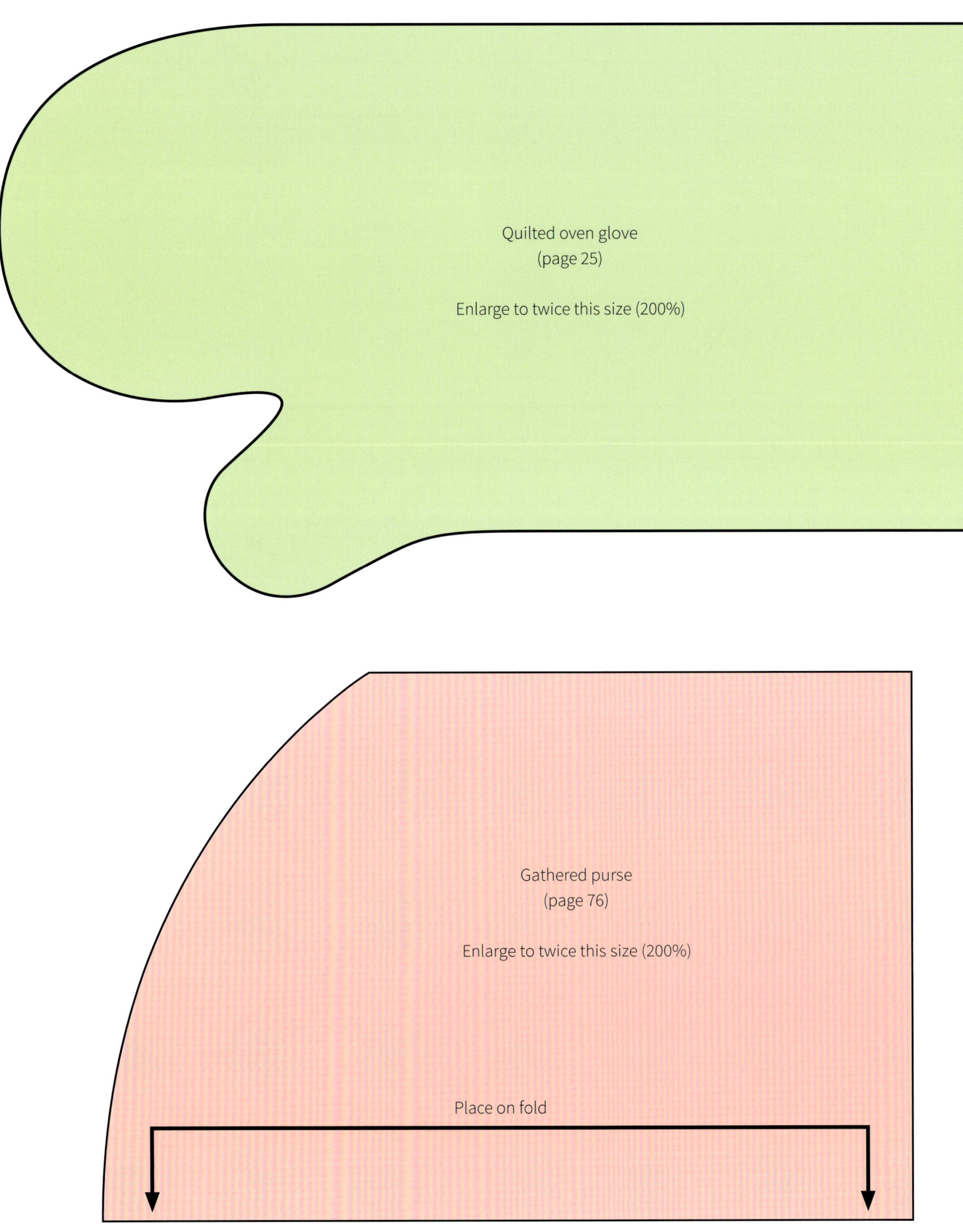
Quilted oven glove
(page 25)
Enlarge to twice this size (200%)
Gathered purse
(page 76)
Enlarge to twice this size (200%)
Place on fold

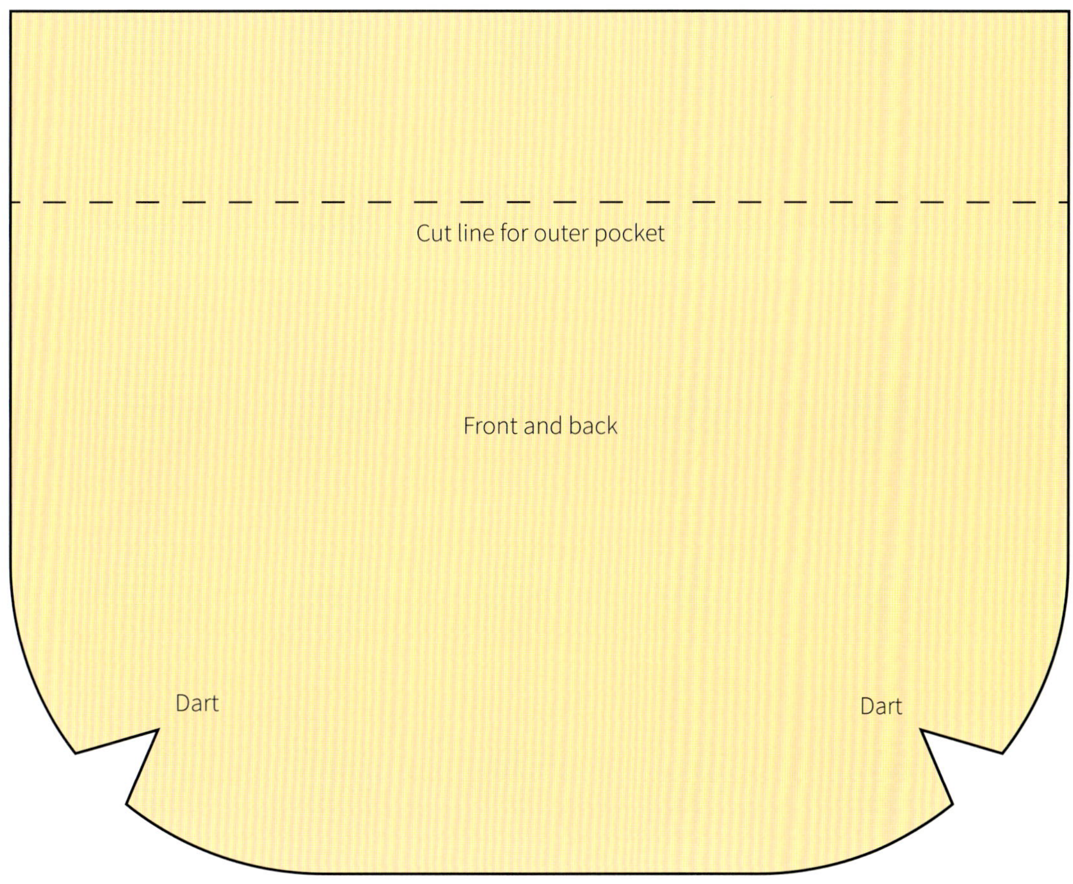

Rounded shoulder bag
(page 89)

Enlarge both templates to twice this size (200%)

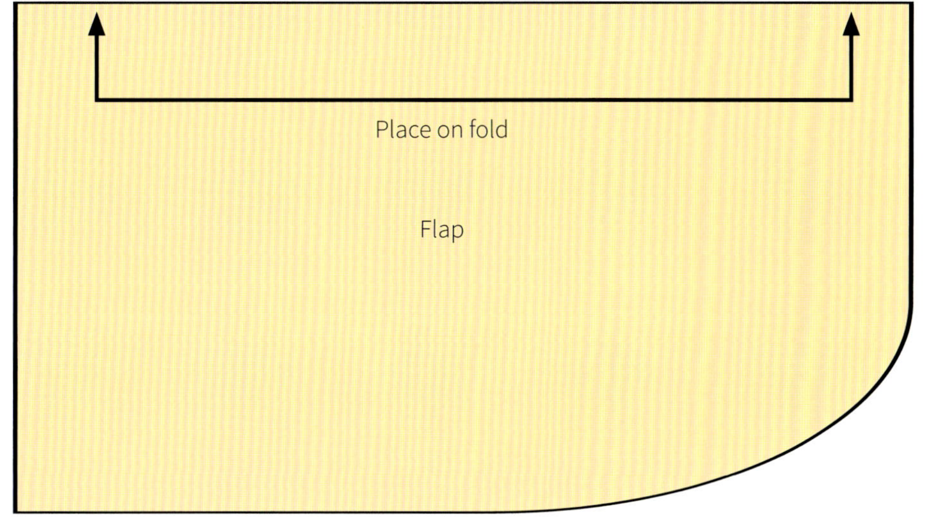

photo transfers

Scan these photo transfer images at 300dpi into your computer and use an image editing program to enlarge them to the size you require. Print them out onto photo-transfer paper to be ironed onto your fabric according to the manufacturer's instructions. The images are backward/reversed because they are ironed on face down and will appear the right way around once they are on your fabric.

Simple coin purse—postcard (page 100)
This image needs to be printed out at 4 x 6in (10 x 15cm)

Mini tote bag—bunting (page 108)
Each piece of bunting needs to be printed out at 2 x 2¼in (5 x 5.5cm)

suppliers

USA and Canada

Art Shack
www.artshack.ca
Canadian supplier of arts and crafts materials and equipment

Dharma Trading Co.
www.dharmatrading.com
Textile craft supplies

Ebay.com
You can find all the printing equipment you need here

Fabric Land
www.fabricland.ca
Large selection of fabrics, with stores across Canada

Hobby Lobby
www.hobbylobby.com
Online arts and crafts store with branches across the US

Michaels
www.michaels.com
Arts and crafts supplier with stores across the USA and Canada

Rex Art
www.rexart.com
Arts and crafts supplies and materials

UK

Abakhan Fabrics, Hobby & Home
www.abakhan.co.uk
Fabric store

Art2ScreenPrint
www.art2screenprint.co.uk
Screen-printing equipment

Atlantis Art
www.atlantisart.co.uk
Lino tools and supplies

Cass Art
www.cassart.co.uk
Print-making supplies

The Cloth House
www.clothhouse.com
Fabrics, vintage buttons, and braids

Ebay.co.uk
You can find all the printing equipment you need here

Fred Aldous Ltd
www.fredaldous.co.uk
Craft materials and fabric paint

George Weil & Sons
www.georgeweil.com
Rubber carving blocks and craft supplies

Handprinted.co.uk
www.handprinted.co.uk
Print-making supplies

Hobbycraft
www.hobbycraft.co.uk
Arts and crafts supplies, fabrics and haberdashery

Intaglio Printmaker
www.intaglioprintmaker.com
Print-making supplies

Ironbridge Fine Arts
www.ironbridgeframing.co.uk
Print-making supplies

Jackson's Art
www.jacksonsart.com
Print-making inks and tools

John Lewis
www.johnlewis.com
Department store with branches across the UK; haberdashery and large range of fabrics

Lawrence Art Supplies
www.tnlawrence.com
Print-making supplies

L. Cornelissen & Son
www.cornelissen.com
Print-making supplies

London Graphic Centre
www.londongraphics.co.uk
Screen-printing and block-printing supplies

Minerva Art Supplies
www.minervaartsupplies.co.uk
Print-making supplies

Rainbow Silks
www.rainbowsilks.co.uk
Wide range of silk fabrics

T N Lawrence & Son Ltd
www.lawrence.co.uk
Print-making supplies

index